CW00557498

DEFEAT SHINY OBJEC

DO THE
~~EASY~~ HARD
THINGS
FIRST

How to Recover from Shiny Object Syndrome, End Self Sabotage, and Turn Chaos into Clarity

#1 INTERNATIONAL BESTSELLING AUTHOR

SCOTT ALLAN

Do the **Hard Things** First:

Defeating Shiny Object Syndrome

*How to Recover from **Shiny Object Syndrome**, **End Self Sabotage**, and Turn **Chaos into Clarity***

More Bestselling Titles From Scott Allan

Empower Your Thoughts

Drive Your Destiny

Relaunch Your Life

The Discipline of Masters

Do the Hard Things First

Undefeated

No Punches Pulled

Fail Big

Rejection Free

Built for Stealth

Check out the complete collection of books and training here:

www.scottallanbooks.com

Do the Hard Things First

Book 4

How to Recover from **Shiny Object Syndrome**, **End Self Sabotage**, and Turn **Chaos into Clarity**

by Scott Allan

Scott Allan
PUBLISHING
ONE BOOK AT A TIME

Copyright © 2024 by **Scott Allan Publishing** all rights reserved.

Do the Hard Things First: Defeating Shiny Object Syndrome by Scott Allan

All rights reserved. No part of this book may be reproduced in any form without permission in writing from the author. Reviewers may quote brief passages in reviews.

While all attempts have been made to verify the information provided in this publication, neither the author nor the publisher assumes any responsibility for errors, omissions, or contrary interpretation of the subject matter herein.

The views expressed in this publication are those of the author alone and should not be taken as expert instruction or commands. The reader is responsible for his or her own actions, as well as his or her own interpretation of the material found within this publication.

Adherence to all applicable laws and regulations, including international, federal, state and local governing professional licensing, business practices, advertising, and all other aspects of doing business in the US, Canada or any other jurisdiction is the sole responsibility of the reader and consumer.

Neither the author nor the publisher assumes any responsibility or liability whatsoever on behalf of the consumer or reader of this material. Any perceived slight of any individual or organization is purely unintentional.

www.scottallanbooks.com

TABLE OF CONTENTS

"People think focus means saying yes to the thing you've got to focus on. But that's not what it means at all. It means saying no to the hundred other good ideas that there are."

— Steve Jobs

Introduction: The Pursuit of Shiny Things

Shiny Object Syndrome is a real thing; it is the downfall of many businesses, business leaders, entrepreneurs and individuals. It turns potentially successful entrepreneurs into overnight failures. It derails your goals and, if practiced without restraint, breaks your mindset by developing bad habits like multitasking and overconsumption.

As consumers, creators, builders and homemakers, it is tempting to want to try everything. We are constantly bombarded with the next best thing, the latest course, and the best kept secrets that are only available for a limited time...limited by how many people want to buy in.

This book you are now reading, Defeating Shiny Object Syndrome, is your #1 blueprint for defeating the enemy that disrupts your work, interrupts your sleep, and destroys your productivity. In this book, you will learn the tactics and strategies for winning over Shiny Object Syndrome, and becoming the greatest version of yourself, both at work and in your personal life.

But first, why I wrote this book.

In late 2020, at the height of the pandemic, I was desperate to generate more growth for my online publishing business and scale to a higher level than I was ready for. I was "looking" for a silver bullet to get me to where I wanted to be, which was generating millions of dollars a year in product and book sales. It was an insatiable goal, and at the time, my ambition far exceeded my talent.

And one of the first lessons I learned is that if you go looking for trouble, you will invariably find that it has been waiting for you all along.

2 · SCOTT ALLAN

But there is another element that is mentioned in this book: keeping up with what everyone else is raving about. If someone has a funnel that is making them thousands of dollars a month, I want to sign up right away to get in on the action.

If they've discovered a new app that helps you lose twenty pounds a month, I'm all in. The chaos of what could be a simple way of life becomes complex when there is no clarity about your goals or direction.

SOS loves to pull you in when you're at your most vulnerable, taking everything it can and leaving you wondering, "What did I get myself into? How did I go from money in the bank to nothing? What was I thinking?"

This thought process destroys your mind. You feel guilty for not knowing better, you feel desperate to correct your mistakes, only to make more of the same mistakes out of a reactive response to fear. Desperation leads to bad choices and that leads to a deeper level of failure and negativity. BY desperately trying to stay afloat, you add more weight that pulls you deeper under.

Do you feel it now? This is how individuals, companies and CEOs fail at work and in life. This is why we must stop listening to the noise and eliminate all distractions.

The book you are about to read is a roadmap to greater freedom. But it's not financial freedom, and I can't promise that your life and business will grow exponentially overnight.

You will be free because the Shiny Object Syndrome will no longer have a hold on your life. You will be able to say NO 99% of the time. You can only say YES after you have thought it through and conclude that YES, this is a worthy investment.

What You Will Learn

As you will learn throughout this book, there is a high price to pay for buying into shiny things that promise a lot but underdeliver. If you're reading this book, you're here for the same reasons I researched and wrote it: I was tired of losing. I was tired of waking up in fear, working harder to make it and paying for things I didn't need, or dealing with the fallout from a deal that could have worked out better if I'd stuck with the original plan.

Taking definitive action does not mean throwing chance to the wind and hoping that good fortune will blow back your way. There are many times when the best course of action is to do nothing. Sit down. Meditate. Think clearly. When you feel anxious, overwhelmed, worried, and scared, these are warning signs to sit still and listen to your fears. Process the negative emotions.

Ask yourself, "Why am I here? Where do I want to be in a year?" Most people fail to do this because our social media, advertising, and options push us to decide now, within ten minutes, before you miss out. And who wants to miss out?

Not me! So, to stay current, to stay in the race, to stay in the game, we fold and we spend and we chase and we rush, but we get very little results...only burnout, frustration, worry, and fearful thinking.

Try this exercise before we begin. I want you to sit quietly for ten minutes. No phone, no timer, no distractions. Turn off the TV. You can do this anywhere, even in a coffee shop. Sit and think and be. Take a deep breath and exhale slowly. Acknowledge where you are in this moment. Ask yourself questions like, "Who am I really? What am I excited about? What am I afraid of?"

If you practice this 2-3 times a day, I promise you that your life will begin to change. Your mindset will change. Your physical appearance will improve. I know this because this one exercise is critical to my daily success.

When I'm running around anxiously, worrying about what's next, wondering if I'll have enough energy to finish those tax returns by noon, the rat race has got me.

Next thing you know, I'm online or in a store looking for a quick fix to numb the pain. I want something to take the edge off. If I just watch one more video, click the buy button again, or grab one more free piece of content attached to someone's email list who will try to upsell me later. I'll start to feel better. But that's not what happens. That's not the happy ending you're going to get, and you realize that's how you got in trouble in the first place.

Stop chasing shiny objects and do the work necessary to achieve your goals, build abundance and focus on what really makes a difference in creating the life you want. Remember: Shiny objects will always derail you IF you don't have clarity about what you're pursuing.

In this book, you will discover a new way of living that will reduce your distractions, eliminate your confusion, reduce and eliminate your stress, and align your actions with your goals.

The stakes of succumbing to distractions and multitasking are high, affecting both professional performance and personal fulfillment. However, through conscious effort and evidence-based strategies, there is hope for regaining focus and achieving sustainable success. Just as John found a path to recovery, so can others by adopting disciplined approaches and fostering an environment that supports their goals.

Ultimately, while distractions will always be a part of life, managing them effectively ensures that we stay on track to achieve our desired results. By balancing engagement with new opportunities and unwavering commitment to primary goals, lasting success becomes not just an aspiration, but a reality.

In this book, I want to explore the signs, symptoms, and negative effects of chasing shiny objects – what I like to call *chasing wild rabbits*. But the beauty of reading this book is that you will discover a new sense of freedom that you've never had before. By understanding how buying into SOS traps ruins your real opportunity, you become free to make better choices.

You begin to trust yourself again, and the sense of loss you had- the loss of personal power-is returned to you 100 times over. As a recovering SOS person, I can share with you first-hand the damage this addictive personality has done and why now, today, is the day you can free yourself from the trap of chasing wild rabbits.

If you're ready to end the madness, let's turn the page and begin...

Your new way of life begins today.

PART 1:

Understanding the Lure of Shiny Object Syndrome

"See yourself living in abundance and you will attract it. It always works, it works every time with every person."

— Bob Proctor

The Impact of Shiny Object Syndrome

In today's world, it's easy to get pulled in multiple directions by the latest trends and innovations. Whether in our personal lives or in our professional endeavors, the temptation to chase after new and exciting opportunities can be overwhelming. This tendency is what we call Shiny Object Syndrome (SOS).

From the lure of a new fitness program to the latest business management tool, shiny objects promise improvement but often distract us from our primary goals.

Shiny Object Syndrome manifests itself in many ways. Imagine you're deeply focused on an important work project when an email about an innovative productivity application suddenly piques your interest. Intrigued by its potential, you spend hours exploring its features, watching tutorials, and configuring settings-all while your original task remains unfinished.

This scenario illustrates how SOS distracts us from critical tasks, resulting in fragmented attention and reduced productivity. The constant pursuit of new opportunities, while tempting, can seriously impede our ability to achieve long-term goals, both personally and professionally.

Explaining the Concept of Shiny Object Syndrome (SOS)

Shiny Object Syndrome (SOS) is a phenomenon in which individuals are constantly distracted by new and exciting opportunities. This relentless pursuit of the next big thing often leads to a scattered approach that causes them to lose sight of essential tasks and long-term goals. In both personal and business contexts, SOS is more common than you might think.

Imagine starting your day with a clear plan to write a critical report, but halfway through, an email about a new marketing tool catches your eye. The tool promises to revolutionize the way you handle customer data. Intrigued, you spend the next few hours learning about its features, signing up for tutorials, and exploring its uses.

At the end of the day, the report remains unfinished, and while you may have learned something new, the essential task that needed your attention has been put on hold. This is the essence of SOS.

Every shiny new object promises improvement or innovation, but can distract us from our primary goals if not managed properly.

Understanding the causes of SOS can help us recognize these distracting tendencies and work to regain control of our focus. Often, SOS is driven by fear of missing out (FOMO). Whether it's a trending technique in your field, a new social media platform, or an innovative piece of software, the allure of being ahead of the curve can be overwhelming.

In addition, the ever-present need for novelty and excitement can make routine tasks feel mundane. Seeking the thrill of the new is a natural human tendency, but if left unchecked, it can lead to fragmented attention and diminished productivity.

Another major driver of SOS is frustration with current tasks. When faced with a challenging project, the temptation to escape into something easier or more exciting is strong. New opportunities offer a temporary reprieve from these frustrations, making them all the more appealing.

Recognizing the signs of Shiny Object Syndrome early is critical. Identifying these distractions can empower you to regain control and effectively prioritize tasks. Consider regular self-assessments to monitor your focus and productivity.

Do you often jump from task to task? Do you leave a lot of projects unfinished? Are you always starting something 'new' but struggle to finish other projects?

If so, it may be time to reevaluate your workflow and implement the strategies we will be learning moving forward.

Managing the distractions of SOS not only improves individual focus, but also promotes organizational efficiency. It allows us to channel our energy into meaningful endeavors, ensuring that our efforts are not scattered, but focused on achieving substantial progress.

Balancing economic growth with human well-being, I believe, requires this disciplined approach, where every decision is carefully weighed against its long-term impact.

So how do we combat SOS effectively? It requires a proactive approach to time management and decision-making, and self-awareness to ensure that the most important tasks are prioritized.

Reclaiming Focus (and Resisting SOS)

Fighting Shiny Object Syndrome starts with deciding to take back control of your mind. When you're able to regain the power of focus, little by little, the lure of the shiny new objects begins to fade. The rest of this book will show you exactly how to identify and correct SOS, but for now, you can begin to regain your focus by fixing one problem area at a time.

#1 - Stay motivated

SOS will affect you more if you're not motivated to do what you're doing in the first place. So, think about how you can become more motivated to complete the task at hand.

Will getting more feedback help? Will breaking the goal into smaller pieces help? Will setting an alarm to work on specific chunks of time help? Will rewarding yourself every time you take a step in the right direction help you stay motivated?

Some people also like to measure their progress - for example, if you wrote 500 words for your new novel last night and made a note of it, you might feel more eager to pick up where you left off this morning.

Another tip that helps some people with their motivation is to know their rhythms and productivity patterns. For example, you may struggle to get work done in the evening, but in the early morning you can get hours of work done in 30 minutes. Knowing your rhythms can help with productivity, and seeing things get done can boost your motivation levels.

#2 – Prioritize Your Tasks

Too often, we try to do too many things at once and end up spreading our energy in multiple directions. If you have a to-do list that you've prioritized, and you decide to approach your day by checking things off the list one at a time, you're less likely to be distracted by shiny objects because you're making it that much easier for yourself to focus.

There are many methods that can work for prioritizing. One popular technique is the Eisenhower Matrix, which involves categorizing all of your tasks into four quadrants: important and urgent tasks, unimportant but urgent tasks, important but not urgent tasks, and not urgent and not important tasks. You can see why it works - you're immediately prompted to focus on what's most important and urgent, and the simplicity of the method makes it easy to incorporate into your daily routine. We will learn this technique in greater detail later on.

You might consider adopting Warren Buffett's "2-list" strategy; it gets you to write down your top 25 goals, then pick just 5 of them, then focus all your attention on those 5 items - because those are the ones you really need to get done.

Another popular prioritization technique is the Ivy Lee method, which asks you to write down your 6 most important tasks for the next day before you leave work each evening. You then rank the tasks so that when you start work the next day, you start with task number 1 - the most important one - and work your way down. You'll be able to tackle things quickly and clearly, one at a time.

#3 – End Procrastination

Procrastination is a focus killer. You push yourself to get something done, but you feel distracted or demotivated. You think about chasing one wild rabbit and then another. You feel a stream of negative thoughts coming up. You feel yourself losing focus. And because you've given yourself the option of putting off critical tasks until the next day - you default to thinking, "It's no big deal, I'll just do it tomorrow!"

This level of thinking continues indefinitely until the cycle is broken, until you can change your thought and action patterns.

If you don't allow yourself to procrastinate, you have no choice but to focus. Yes, negative thoughts will always enter your mind. Distractions will tempt you. But since you can't put off the work at hand, you will push them out of your mind. You will guard your mind against the forces that move in to derail your efforts.

If you need to, slow down for a moment and take a few deep breaths. Some people also keep a journal to write down any negative or distracting thoughts. Once your thoughts are on paper and you feel calmer about your vision and intentions, get back to the task at hand.

#4 - Stop Multitasking

When you try to juggle too much work at once, you don't give yourself the opportunity to truly immerse yourself in something that can be interesting, engaging, enlightening, or fun - so you make it easier for shiny new things to hijack your attention and introduce the anarchy of distraction and confusion into your mind.

When you stop multitasking - and make a conscious decision to focus on one thing at a time - chances are you'll be immersed in what you're supposed to be doing. Once you're in the zone, you'll build the momentum to move forward. For this to happen, you must maintain a clean calendar and a manageable, well-sequenced to-do list with a clear set of actions leading to your desired outcome.

Multitasking is an illusion, and it will only distract you from your true purpose. The human mind is designed to stay fixed and focused on one thing. Anything more than that and we burn up our resources by draining energy and bringing chaos back into our day.

#5 - Remove Temptations

Distraction isn't just about lack of focus - it's about allowing yourself to shift your focus to something else over and over again.

Why not clean up the clutter and make your physical and digital environment more conducive to focus? Why not block out the constant temptation to chase after more things that are bigger, better, and brighter?

If you can put yourself in the right environment, things will automatically become easier to accomplish. You could turn off all notifications while you sleep. You could put your phone on silent mode or just turn it off. You have to get into the habit of turning things off to help yourself focus on a deeper level.

The Core of SOS (and Your Mission)

At its core, SOS is about fear, distraction, and prioritizing what matters most. The more you can get yourself to want to focus and be able to focus, the less power distractions will have over you. So, let yourself wonder and explore - but when the time comes, make sure you are able to focus your attention and bring it fully into the present moment.

You need to show up for yourself and be ready to give your absolute best. This means approaching your work, relationships, and personal goals with a clear sense of direction. Anything that distracts you from your true intentions will not help you get there, but will derail the path you should be taking.

Do you click the buy button for an item you don't need to get a dopamine rush? Are you turning on Netflix because you're bored and have forgotten what's important for today? Are you mindlessly texting and scrolling because it's fun and someone is paying attention to your online activity with likes and emoticons?

What really matters is **who you want to be in the future**, and **what you're willing to do to get there**.

That's it.

Be aware of the empty activities that cause your mind to default to a failed set of actions. Train your mind to recognize when you fall into a "shiny object" black hole. It probably happens several times a day when you lose precious minutes and hours in mindless funk. When you see it happening, you can stop it.

You're not powerless, you're powerful; you're not afraid, you're fearless.

The rest of this book will teach you how to develop the clarity, confidence, and perseverance to say no to everything that gets in your way. Instead of giving your attention to a distraction, you will redirect that energy toward your goals and your determination to achieve your greatest aspirations.

With a clear focus, you become unstoppable.

Why we Focus on Shiny New Objects

Most of us understand the importance of focus in achieving a worthwhile goal. Whenever we think of past success, we can usually attribute it to focused thoughts, energies, decisions, and actions over a sustained period of time.

So why does SOS affect us? Why do shiny new objects appeal to us mature, educated, successful, experienced adults?

Our environment doesn't help. We live in a world where chasing shiny objects is the norm. We're surrounded by constant triggers designed to attract the consumer in us. We're drowning in a barrage of emails, WhatsApps, text messages, Slack chats, Zoom calls, iWatch alerts, Instagram rolls, and Tweets - hardly an environment conducive to focus.

What research tells us about the allure of shiny new objects

We know that different parts of our brains respond to different stimuli around us to help us make sense of the world.

Scientists have long known that there are two different ways the human brain processes information from the outside world. There's "automatic focus," like paying attention when a smoke alarm goes off, which creates "bottom-up" signals in the brain. And there's "intentional focus," like when you look at a painting, which creates "top-down" signals in the brain.

What's more, recent research from MIT shows us that these signals come from different parts of the brain, and that neural activity is "faster for automatic stimuli and slower for things we choose to pay attention to. It goes on to explain that anything that stands out to the brain as different - like a red car in a sea of yellow taxis - will grab our attention and trigger an automatic or "bottom-up" response.

In other words, distractions and shiny new objects activate a different part of our brain than the rest of the brain that's responsible for our daily norm, and they do so at a higher frequency. That's why the lure is so powerful. That's why it's hard for us to focus - with SOS there's a whole different mental mechanism kicking in and demanding attention. The different parts of the brain that are activated by and for different responses need to be balanced, and the dominant frequencies need to be turned down.

A constantly distracted mind also feeds a kind of unhappiness-distraction loop. All the effects of SOS may not be direct or immediate, but what we don't realize is that it's harder to be happy when our mind is constantly distracted or wandering.

On average, people spend nearly 47% of their waking hours thinking about what's not going on-that's how distracted we are in general. That's how much we think about what may never happen, the past, the future, or shiny new objects, all put together.

Many spiritual practitioners, religions, and philosophies prove that presence, or mindfulness, is a necessity for happiness. To be happy, you must live in the now. You can't do that by chasing after every shiny new object.

20 Ways Chasing Random Opportunities Sabotages Your Life

Here are ten ways in which the pursuit of random opportunities, or "Shiny Object Syndrome" (SOS), can sabotage your success, well-being, and overall life satisfaction.

From creating stress and anxiety to developing a scarcity mindset and losing credibility, SOS can lead you down a path of unfulfilled dreams and missed opportunities. Learn how to recognize and avoid these pitfalls to stay focused and achieve lasting success.

1: **You create stress and anxiety.** SOS consumes a lot of your energy. It makes you run in circles; the rush of the new chase may seem exciting for a while, but as soon as it wears off, you're back where you started. The moment you hit a roadblock, you may become frustrated, anxious, and demotivated.

2: **You lose money.** If you run a business, you know that the essence of it is how you manage every last dollar. If you're chasing wild rabbits and backing them with real investment dollars just because they're the shiny new thing, you're bound to lose money.

Too many entrepreneurs jump too quickly into projects without proper research or proof of success, and they leave what they started unfinished, costing their company and themselves thousands of dollars in the process. Even in cases where they don't directly invest and lose money, they do so indirectly through lost productivity, morale and resource time.

3: **You develop a scarcity mindset.** People driven by SOS generally have a scarcity mindset. They feel the need to chase that shiny object before someone else gets it, or before they're left out. The scarcity mindset makes people think that everything in life is finite, whether it is objects, money, people, or opportunities. They feel anxious and eager to jump on the next thing because they don't want to miss out on what others will have while they won't. With SOS, you're focused on limitations and unable to see the abundance of what you already have.

4: **You reduce your decision-making confidence and lose your credibility.** Let's say you're a team leader - you're in charge of a project and your juniors, seniors and peers are watching. If you keep chasing the next idea and setting the next goal at the expense of the current one, your indecisiveness not only hinders the progress of your project, but also causes you to lose credibility. You may stress out and confuse your team. And in the long run, you may lose confidence in your own decision-making.

5: You can't finish what you start. A classic effect of SOS is that nothing ever gets finished. People with SOS are often chronic "starters" - proposing new projects, finding new markets to expand into, planning new trips, making new friends, discovering new things to invest in, buying the latest trendy item, or pursuing a new romantic interest.

Of course, starting any of these endeavors is great. But starting a new endeavor at the expense of an existing one, or without adequate reflection, very often just because "everyone else is doing it," is harmful. You miss out on both the new thing and what you've already got.

6: You pay a high price for missed opportunities. When you focus on shiny new things, you don't put enough time and energy into developing what you started. That idea you had might have been worth something great if you'd just given yourself a chance to work it through. You might have come up with a series of iterations that could have resulted in a wonderful new development and a viable business. SOS makes you pay a very high opportunity cost.

7: You develop mental fatigue and disrupt your productivity. SOS comes from a constant stream of shiny new distractions. And when you're distracted, you can't be productive. When you're looking at the new thing, you're not focused on the thing that should be getting your time and attention. And so the thing that needs to get done takes longer and longer to get done. In this way, chasing wild rabbits over and over will eventually leave you feeling exhausted.

8: You will continue to feel unfulfilled and end up with a poor quality of life. Chasing after every shiny new thing on your radar can also mean that you begin to place undue importance on objects, forgetting how valuable the real experiences and people in your life are.

If the chase goes unchecked, you may lose touch with what you really need and what really makes you happy. You may become addicted to objects instead of appreciating people. You may become insensitive or unbalanced as a person. You may begin to neglect your responsibilities. You may develop an obsession with the "new" at the expense of the "real. And you may end up with a life that feels unfulfilled and empty.

9: **You can't set clear responsibilities and delegate**. If you're personally obsessed with pursuing something, you're unlikely to do so with an objective, unbiased, and practical frame of mind. You're more likely to want to "do it all yourself" rather than delegate the pursuit to the right people with the right resources. Delegation is essential to success-especially in business.

10: **You make your problems bigger**. The pursuit of a shiny new object can make you obsessive and overconfident. When you start working with blinders on, refusing to evaluate multiple potential growth paths or consequences with an open mind, you're on your way to digging your own grave.

11. **Erodes Long-term Vision and Goals**. Constantly shifting focus to new opportunities can erode your long-term vision and goals. When you're perpetually chasing the latest trend or idea, it becomes difficult to maintain a coherent strategy for your future. This lack of long-term planning can hinder your ability to achieve significant milestones and sustain success.

12. **Damages Relationships**. The instability and inconsistency caused by SOS can spill over into your personal relationships. Friends, family, and colleagues may find it challenging to trust and rely on someone who is always jumping from one pursuit to another. This can lead to strained relationships, misunderstandings, and a lack of meaningful connections.

13. **Increases Stress and Burnout**. The constant pursuit of new opportunities can lead to chronic stress and eventual burnout. The never-ending cycle of starting new projects without seeing

them through to completion can be mentally and physically exhausting. Over time, this relentless pace can take a toll on your health and overall well-being.

14. Hinders Skill Development. Focusing on too many different areas prevents you from honing your skills in any one domain. Mastery requires dedicated practice and time, and SOS can prevent you from gaining the deep expertise needed to excel. This can limit your professional growth and the value you can offer to others.

15. Reduces Financial Stability. Frequently diverting resources to new ventures can drain your financial reserves. Investing in unproven opportunities without proper due diligence can lead to significant financial losses. This lack of financial stability can create additional stress and limit your ability to invest in truly valuable opportunities in the future.

16. Creates Inconsistency in Brand or Personal Identity. If you're an entrepreneur or a professional, SOS can lead to inconsistencies in your brand or personal identity. Constantly changing directions can confuse your audience or clients, making it difficult for them to understand what you stand for or offer. A clear, consistent message is crucial for building trust and loyalty.

17. Promotes Procrastination. Paradoxically, SOS can become a form of procrastination. By continually chasing new opportunities, you might be avoiding the hard work required to see your current projects through to completion. This avoidance behavior can prevent you from making meaningful progress and achieving your goals.

18. Weakens Team Cohesion. If you're part of a team or leading one, SOS can weaken team cohesion and morale. Frequent changes in direction can confuse and frustrate team members, leading to decreased productivity and engagement. A clear, stable vision is essential for maintaining a motivated and unified team.

19. **Undermines Personal Satisfaction and Happiness.** The constant pursuit of new opportunities can undermine your personal satisfaction and happiness. True fulfillment often comes from seeing a project through to completion and reaping the rewards of your hard work. By continually abandoning projects, you miss out on the sense of accomplishment and joy that comes from finishing what you start.

20. **Increases Likelihood of Failure.** Finally, SOS increases the likelihood of failure. By spreading yourself too thin and not giving adequate attention to any single project, you reduce your chances of success. Focus and perseverance are key to achieving significant outcomes, and SOS can derail these essential components of success.

The relentless pursuit of random opportunities can have profound and far-reaching consequences on various aspects of your life. From creating stress and financial instability to damaging relationships and hindering skill development, the costs of SOS are significant. It undermines your long-term vision, reduces your credibility, and can even lead to burnout.

To achieve lasting success and fulfillment, it's essential to recognize these pitfalls and cultivate focus, consistency, and a gratitude-based mindset.

In this book, you will learn the tactics and strategies for building your own blueprint to wage war against your greatest enemy when it comes to killing the lure of Shiny Object Syndrome—that enemy is yourself.

The Role of Dopamine and Social Conditioning

In this hyper-connected age, distractions are everywhere. Notifications ping on our phones, emails flood our inboxes, and social media beckons with endless updates. These constant intrusions do more than interrupt our tasks; they shape our brain chemistry and behavior in subtle but significant ways. The struggle to stay focused isn't just a battle against external factors; it's also an internal battle involving our own psychological makeup.

One of the key reasons we find distractions so compelling is the role of dopamine, a neurotransmitter associated with pleasure and reward. Each notification or "like" triggers a dopamine release, creating fleeting moments of satisfaction that lure us into repetitive behavior.

Imagine working on an important report when your phone buzzes with a new message. This brief interruption releases dopamine provides instant gratification, but ultimately derails your focus and productivity. This cycle illustrates how short-term rewards often override long-term goals, leaving us perpetually distracted.

In this chapter, we will explore the psychological underpinnings of distraction, focusing on the role of dopamine and social conditioning in shaping our attention spans. You'll learn about dopamine's powerful influence on our behavior and strategies for managing its effects to regain control of your focus.

We'll also explore how societal norms contribute to our distraction habits, examining how modern culture glorifies busyness and instant connectivity. By understanding these dynamics, you can implement practical techniques to increase your productivity and maintain sustained attention amidst the constant barrage of distractions.

Dopamine's Role in Distraction

Dopamine, often referred to as the "pleasure chemical," is a vital neurotransmitter that plays an important role in our brain's reward system. It's responsible for the feelings of euphoria and satisfaction we get from activities we find pleasurable or rewarding, like eating delicious food, receiving praise, or even scrolling through social media. This neural circuit drives us toward novelty and instant gratification, making it a double-edged sword when it comes to maintaining focus and avoiding distractions.

When we get a "hit" of dopamine, our brain registers pleasure, which then motivates us to repeat the behavior that caused it. This cycle can lead to distracting behaviors as we constantly seek quick rewards instead of focusing on long-term goals. For example, checking your phone every few minutes may give you a moment's pleasure, but it disrupts your overall productivity.

Recognizing this cycle is the first step to mastering it. By becoming aware of dopamine-driven urges, individuals can begin to implement strategies to manage these impulses. One powerful technique is delayed gratification.

Delayed gratification involves resisting the temptation of an immediate reward in favor of a greater, later benefit. This approach can help you resist distractions and focus on tasks that lead to long-term success.

Here are some things you can do to get on track:

- Start by setting clear, achievable long-term goals to provide motivation beyond immediate rewards.
- Whenever you feel the urge for a quick dopamine hit, remind yourself of the larger goal you are working toward.

- Practice small acts of delayed gratification daily, such as waiting to check your notifications until you have completed a task.

Establishing periods of limited exposure to immediate rewards, also known as dopamine detoxes, can significantly impact your ability to focus. A dopamine detox doesn't mean cutting off all sources of pleasure-rather, it means consciously limiting engagement in activities that provide instant gratification, such as social media, video games, or snacking. Instead, make time for activities that offer more substantial, longer-lasting rewards.

During a **dopamine detox**, you might do the following:

- Set specific times during the day when you allow yourself to check your phone or social media.
- Engage in other forms of entertainment that don't rely on screens, such as reading a book, exercising, or spending time outdoors.
- Keep a journal of your experiences and note any changes in your focus and productivity.

Practicing mindfulness is another powerful tool to counteract dopamine-driven distractions. Mindfulness helps you stay present and fully engaged in the task at hand, rather than succumbing to the lure of instant gratification.

Activities like meditation, deep breathing, or even mindful walking can train your brain to appreciate the moment without constantly seeking external stimuli.

You can incorporate mindfulness into your routine by:

- Starting your day with a five-minute meditation session to set a calm, focused tone.
- Practicing deep work by dedicating uninterrupted blocks of time to intensive tasks, free from potential distractions.

- Paying conscious attention to mundane tasks, such as washing dishes or taking a shower, to cultivate the habit of being present.

The benefits of understanding dopamine's role in our distraction behaviors go far beyond improved concentration. It's about gaining autonomy over your mental landscape, ensuring that you are the one steering your cognitive ship rather than being at the mercy of fleeting whims. This awareness allows you to make deliberate choices that better align with your long-term goals, whether they're related to career advancement, personal development, or academic success.

By managing dopamine's influence, you regain control of your attention. You become aware of what triggers your need for instant gratification and can consciously choose activities that support long-term gains. Understanding and manipulating your dopamine cycle isn't about denying yourself pleasure; it's about redirecting your neural responses toward what will truly enrich your life in the long run.

Let's take a practical example. Say you're working on an important project that requires deep concentration. From time to time, you may feel the urge to check your phone or browse the Internet. This action triggers a release of dopamine that gives you a brief sense of satisfaction, but ultimately derails your progress.

By recognizing these tendencies, you can set aside specific breaks and dedicate them to checking messages or surfing the web. Over time, your brain will realize that it can get its dopamine fix, but only at certain times, which will help you sustain longer periods of focused work.

Remember, the goal isn't to eliminate all sources of dopamine, but to regulate its influence on your productivity. A balanced approach ensures that you reap the benefits of this powerful neurotransmitter without falling prey to its potential pitfalls. The art is in moderation, in structuring your environment and habits to support sustained attention rather than sporadic bursts of unfocused activity.

It is impossible to overstate the importance of such practices in shaping a productive, fulfilling life. As a busy professional, entrepreneur, or student, the challenge is to balance immediate pleasures with long-term accomplishments.

By wisely harnessing the power of dopamine, you're not just improving your focus-you're investing in a mindset that prioritizes growth, resilience, and robust mental health. This balance is critical to navigating the complexities of modern life, where distractions abound and demands on our time are ever-increasing.

By understanding and managing dopamine, you'll be better equipped to deal with the pressures and challenges of your daily life. You will gain not only productivity, but also a deeper sense of fulfillment and purpose-qualities that, in the grand scheme of things, are infinitely more rewarding than the brief highs provided by immediate gratification.

The 50-point Shiny Object Syndrome Evaluation

By now, I'm sure you can identify some of the signs and symptoms of SOS from what you've read so far. This chapter will help you delve deeper into your diagnosis of SOS and teach you how to identify exactly what is causing you to chase shiny objects.

Chasing shiny objects is a common phenomenon; we all do it. And while experimenting with new things and fully exploring what life has to offer is a wonderful attitude to have, it becomes harmful when taken too far. Chasing shiny objects comes at the expense of your present life, and when it becomes an addiction, you've gone too far.

In our daily lives, we're surrounded by examples of chasing shiny objects. Consider if any of the following sound familiar:

- You just bought a new line of clothes for your wardrobe, even though you still haven't taken the price tags off the last ones you bought.
- You just joined a gym and have a trainer-prescribed routine, but someone recommended that you try this new fitness program that worked for their friend, so you jump ship.
- Experimenting with a new diet when your nutritionist has already given you a health plan that's only a few weeks old.
- You jump from relationship to relationship. With each partner, you disagree, fight, and look for more - so you move on to another partner who seems like a better match. Before you know it, it's the same story all over again.
- Your current job pays well, has exciting prospects and supportive colleagues - but the new startup on the block is

hiring, everyone's clamoring to get in, and they offer better perks, so you decide to quit.

- You can't seem to stick with your current investment strategy - you want to get in on what seems to be the latest and hottest investment.

We chase shiny objects, not only in our personal lives, but also in business. You've probably seen the following in entrepreneurs around you (or in yourself)

- Someone tells you about a new idea - a patent or a prototype - and now that's all you seem to be interested in.
- A new market suddenly looks very attractive, while tried-and-true playgrounds for your business have lost their appeal despite their practicality.
- Your friend's company is using a new software that promises instant sales increases, so you want it too.
- Your competitor's marketing and advertising tactics seem to be working, so you want to emulate them.
- You believe in multitasking at work, and you expect your team to multitask, too.

As you've probably noticed, some signs of Shiny Object Syndrome are subtle and very common-it takes honest introspection and a genuine desire to focus on your own path to break the habit of chasing new things.

Here's a comprehensive questionnaire to help you better assess your SOS affliction. Once you have completed this assessment, you will have a clear understanding of where you stand in your relationship with the pursuit of shiny objects. More importantly, the rest of this book is designed to help you break it.

Recognize the Signs: Your 50-point SOS Test

Here are the most common signs and symptoms of shiny object syndrome; if you tend to run after anything that shines, you'll be able to identify with at least half of the items on this list. Make a note of the prompts and categories that you answer with a resounding "yes"-and that's where you'll want to focus your distraction-fighting efforts.

Workplace and Professional SOS

1. Are you always on your cell phone at work? (Surveys on workplace distractions show that 44% of employees say that browsing the Internet is their biggest distraction at work).
2. Do you find it necessary to scan your social media feed several times a day and reply to your DMs immediately?
3. Do you feel the need to open and reply to every email as soon as it hits your inbox?
4. Are you unable to concentrate on the task at hand (e.g. writing a report) when you see your colleagues hanging around the coffee machine? (37% of employees cite office gossip as the top distraction that keeps them from focusing).
5. Do you find yourself taking multiple coffee or snack breaks throughout the day?
6. Do you find yourself stopping frequently to chat with a colleague who walks by? (27% of employees say the biggest distraction they face at work is colleagues interrupting them to chat).
7. Do you tend to lock yourself away (e.g., in your cubicle) so that you can concentrate fully on the task at hand until it is completed, even if it means skipping meals or important coaching sessions?
8. Have you bought several website domain names but never built or launched any of the sites?
9. Do you jump from one business idea to another with your dream and vision in your head instead of putting it down on paper?
10. Do you often change your work routine to accommodate something new you're trying out, such as a new cycling hobby?

11. Are you tired of starting new projects and never finishing any?

12. Do you have a reputation for being a 'dreamer' or 'talker' but not known for your follow-through?

13. Do you spend all day jumping from one goal to another without seeing any of them fulfilled?

14. Do you find that you're not taken seriously at work because you're known for changing your mind or being indecisive?

15. Are you unable to complete most of your tasks on time?

16. Do you ignore writing down your to-do list? Do you find that you never stick to the list you make day after day?

17. Do you have trouble prioritizing your work?

18. Do you feel you have no choice but to multitask given the number of things you have on your plate?

19. Have you become accustomed to expecting everyone to perform multiple business activities simultaneously?

20. Do you find yourself constantly enrolling in a new course to improve your skills, but never seem to be able to apply any of it to your work?

SOS in your Social and Personal Life

21. Do you find yourself saying "yes" to things that come up during the day, regardless of what you thought you'd be doing that day?

22. Are you afraid that if you say "no" to something, such as a group invitation, you won't be asked again?

23. Do you feel surprised, upset, or angry when you see updates on news you think you should have known about or things you wish you had been a part of?

24. In general, do you feel dissatisfied with your life?

25. Do you feel the need to constantly compare your life to others, such as by constantly scrolling through social media to find areas where you're doing better?

26. Do you feel the need to live a fast-paced lifestyle and perhaps worry when things slow down? For example, you may feel

the need to know exactly when and where you're going to travel next, or what your next hobby will be - not because you want to try new things, but because you're always trying to fill a void.

27. Do you find it extremely important that others think well of you in many or all areas of your life, such as your job performance, financial status, travel, family, choice of partner, choice of friends, clothes, hair, makeup, background, body image, the things you own, and your overall lifestyle?

28. Are you easily overwhelmed, stressed, or depressed?

29. Do you feel a constant need to be surrounded by others-be they your friends, classmates, or coworkers-because you're afraid of being left out or alone?

30. Are you often made fun of for your poor health habits - such as lack of sleep or fatigue? Do you constantly feel physically, mentally, or emotionally exhausted and like you just can't keep up with everything you need to do?

31. Are you easily distracted or absent-minded when it comes to everyday tasks, such as driving a car?

32. Do you generally feel that you're not worthy of what you want? Or that others are more worthy than you?

33. Do you feel inadequate compared to your peers, or that you can't do things as well as they can? Do you feel that you don't respect yourself?

34. Do you feel that you lack strengths, good qualities, or that you don't have much to offer?

35. Do you keep looking for new "things" even though you don't understand why - just to have something new to rave about?

SOS in Overvaluing Objects

36. Are you afraid of missing out on a product you like, so you tend to act immediately to get it?

37. If you did a quick scan of everything you own, would you say you've never used most of it?

38. Do you feel the need to keep buying things even though you know you may never use them?

39. Do you find yourself easily immersed in advertising - for example, while scrolling through your Instagram feed or while driving your car?

40. Once you like something, are you so focused on it that you can't concentrate on anything else until you buy it?

41. Do you tend to borrow other people's trendy items if you can't get your hands on them?

42. Are you afraid of new things because you might get too attached to them?

43. Do you constantly buy new things that are really just different versions of the same thing?

44. Have you found yourself buying things before you understand what exactly they do or how exactly they work, just because you're enamored by their appeal?

45. Do you believe that other people are what they own, i.e., that people are measured or judged by their possessions? Do you like to associate only with people of the same social status, or do you feel it is a must to maintain a glamorous lifestyle?

46. Do you believe that your identity is inextricably linked to what you own, and that you therefore need to own the best things?

47. Do you feel a lack of goals, challenges or purpose in your life that you believe can be filled with things?

48. Do you value things over people? Or objects over experiences?

49. Do you have a hard time throwing things away even though you know you'll never use or need them?

50. In general, do you have difficulty letting go?

The 50-Point Test Scoring System

Each "yes" answer is worth 1 point. After completing the test, add up your total score to determine the severity of your Shiny Object Syndrome (SOS). Here's how to interpret your score:

0-10 points: Low susceptibility to SOS. You generally stay focused and manage distractions well.

11-20 points: Moderate susceptibility to SOS. Some areas need improvement, but you have good control over your focus.

21-30 points: High susceptibility to SOS. You often struggle with distractions and may need to implement several strategies to improve your focus.

31-40 points: Very high susceptibility to SOS. Distractions significantly impact your productivity and personal life. Urgent action is needed to manage SOS.

41-50 points: Extreme susceptibility to SOS. Distractions are severely impacting all areas of your life. Immediate and comprehensive action is required to regain control.

Now add up your score. Here is where you stand in the breakdown of your score.

With this questionnaire, you've identified the severity of your SOS and narrowed down the areas you need to focus on to confront and combat it.

That's what the rest of this book will help you do: **How to Defeat Shiny Object Syndrome**!

PART 2:

The Mindset Traps of Shiny Object Syndrome

"If you don't pay appropriate attention to what has your attention, it will take more of your attention than it deserves."

—*David Allen*

Introduction

Shiny Object Syndrome can be triggered by a variety of emotions and thought patterns. In this section, we will discuss the emotional triggers that can contribute to Shiny Object Syndrome. Correcting just one of these triggers can and will reduce your risk of falling into the trap.

These emotional triggers are all interrelated, and one feeds into the other. But remember: This is a journey of recovery, and healing takes time. You must be patient with yourself and take action on the small things that have a leverage effect.

In the end, it is our avoidance that keeps us from facing reality and escaping fear. But if you do one hard thing first every day, you can increase your intrinsic value by 1% with every effort.

A brief overview...

The Sunk Cost Fallacy

The Sunk Cost Fallacy is a cognitive bias in which individuals continue to invest in a project, decision, or relationship because of the cumulative prior investment (time, money, effort), even when it would be more rational to cut losses and move on. This fallacy occurs because people focus on past costs that cannot be recouped, rather than on the future benefits of different decisions. It leads to poor decision making because people become irrationally committed to a failed course of action.

FOMO: Fear of missing out

This is the feeling of anxiety or worry that arises when we think that others may be having experiences or opportunities that we aren't. It's driven by a fear of social rejection or a desire to maintain social status.

FOBO: Fear of Better Options (FOBO)

This is the fear or anxiety that comes from having too many options and feeling paralyzed by the prospect of making the wrong choice. It's driven by the fear of making the wrong choice or regretting a decision.

The Impact of Multitasking and Shiny Object Syndrome

Multitasking and Shiny Object Syndrome (SOS) are closely related because they both involve a lack of sustained focus. SOS occurs when individuals constantly chase new, exciting opportunities, much like multitasking involves jumping between tasks. Both behaviors prevent the completion of important tasks and contribute to a fragmented, unproductive workflow.

Now, you will learn about the four mindset traps of Shiny Object Syndrome...

Shiny Object Syndrome: Mindset Traps

What are the psychological triggers of SOS? Why and how do we get caught up in chaos? What fuels our attraction to shiny objects? And how do we keep getting stuck in the SOS unhappiness loop?

We know that we tend to feel distracted when we lack clarity and confidence in what we're trying to do. When we're not fully immersed and invested in achieving our goals, SOS tends to have a stronger hold.

In pursuit of a goal, we may lack the skills we need, feel unmotivated, or be frustrated with our goals and the pace of our progress - all of which make it easier to give in to the lure of the shiny new object.

This is how it starts - and once started, SOS is perpetuated by certain psychological triggers, some around us and some within us.

Identifying these triggers and understanding why they keep you in an SOS mindset can help you break free. Here is a short list of the nine ways we fall into the Shiny Object Syndrome trap.

#1 - The Interrupt Marketing Trap

We're so used to interrupt marketing that we don't even think about it. Maybe you've searched for something on Google and it keeps popping up in your Instagram feed - you're probably used to it by now. And you're probably indifferent to getting tons of spam emails and cold calls.

Interruption marketing is all around us, constantly feeding our SOS. The average person now sees over 2,000 outbound marketing interruptions every day - across multiple media, including phone calls, emails, radio, TV, and social media. You were just thinking about traveling somewhere, and now you're seeing that one hotel over and over again, being lured into action.

It's up to you to see that it's all about marketing. And it's up to you to find creative ways to block out all the distractions.

How do you get out of the marketing interrupt trap?

#1 - Set boundaries.

There are many tools to help you do this. You can use caller ID. You can set up spam filters. And you can limit the time you spend on social media. Setting limits on your energy and time is essential if you want to stop chasing shiny objects.

It's simply not possible to say yes to every opportunity that comes your way without getting overwhelmed and burnt out. What are the outcomes that really make you happy? That should be up to you, not the companies with the best marketing strategies.

#2 - The Artificial Scarcity Trap - "It's the last one left!"

Artificial scarcity is becoming more and more common. We've always had limited editions, and we're used to them. When brands create a sense of limited supply - true or false - it works. It works because people want what only they can have and others can't.

What we don't often realize is that the scarcity mindset that brands create is mostly artificial - they create a sense of limited supply to get you to act fast. Artificial scarcity is excellent fuel when it comes to feeding Shiny Object Syndrome; it's not just a shiny object you're chasing - it's the last one!

It's the last dress in line!

It's the last room at the hotel!

It's the last seat at that free webinar.

It's the last limited edition item - limited to how many people you can sell it to.

That's not to say there's anything wrong with owning or trying things from a limited-edition collection. There's nothing wrong with buying a rare pink diamond. Or trying the Starbucks Unicorn Frappuccino that sold out in a day. Or buying one of only 10,000 NFTs by an artist whose work you really like. It's not bad, as long as you find real value in what you're investing in - not just because you're being tricked into it as part of a sales strategy.

How do you get out of the scarcity trap? By asking yourself, "Will I value this item in a few months?" Or, "When I think about this a year from now, will I be glad I did/bought this?"

#3 - The Urgency Trap - "Buy this now, now, now!" or "Do this now, now, now!"

All that glitters is not gold - but it is marketed as gold. And if you're an easy target, like someone with an SOS - that is, if you're easily persuaded by the lure of all that glitters - you'll stay in the trap.

Marketing has evolved, and with the help of tons of research, brands know exactly how to get you to act the way they want you to. They know how to instill the fear of FOMO. They know how to make the buying process frictionless. They even know which colors to use to create a warm environment and evoke a sense of trust. And they know how to put a deadline on their sale, because if they make you want to buy "now, now!" you probably will.

Of course, SOS isn't limited to customers - it's also common among professionals and entrepreneurs. If you don't think you fall into the urgency trap at work, think again. How often have you stopped doing what you should be doing in order to do some other, seemingly more interesting task, perhaps one that provides a sense of instant gratification?

How do you get out of the urgency trap? You stop and think; do you really need to have or do this thing right now? And next, do you need to have or do this thing at all?

#4 - The FOMO Trap - "I'm the only one who doesn't have it..."

FOMO affects kids and adults, entrepreneurs and travelers, managers and students - it affects everyone in everything, if you let it. If you repeatedly feel like you're the only one missing out on the things that matter, whatever they may be, you're likely to live with extreme unhappiness, feelings of inferiority, loneliness, anxiety, and even depression.

The best way to beat the FOMO trap is to develop and maintain a strong internal belief system. When you know your worth and what you value, you will not place undue importance on the shiny things around you. You will not find much meaning in constantly comparing yourself to others. You will not complain when you are grateful for what you have. You'll be confident and immersed in your own path. Your self-esteem will improve. And you'll be busy focusing on what makes you happy and how to get more of it.

#5 - The Insufficiency Trap - "I'm Not Enough

We've all felt like we weren't enough or didn't measure up in some aspect of life. Many things fuel the SOS - emotional shame, boredom, anxiety, fatigue, frustration, depression, fear of uncertainty, and feelings of inadequacy.

When you feel like you're not enough, it's also easier to believe that getting some of the shiny new things around you will make you feel good enough, or at least make others feel good enough. But it's a trap - it doesn't work that way.

That sense of worth can only come from within. No one outside of you can tell you who you are, what you should want, or what you deserve. And when you operate with a high sense of self-worth, you'll demand the best for yourself - and the inadequacy trap will no longer work.

#6 - The Lost Opportunity Trap

We're so affected by the SOS because we're afraid of losing good opportunities. Why not go after this one? What if we don't get another one? The SOS affects us because we think (wrongly) that opportunities are scarce. We forget that opportunity, like beauty, is in the eye of the beholder.

To avoid the lost-opportunity trap when responding to an SOS trigger, ask yourself, "Will this be as important in three months? If the answer is yes, then maybe you really do care about pursuing the specific opportunity in front of you, and you should. If the answer is no or maybe, it might be okay to let it go.

Stop seeing opportunities as limited - they're not. Life is about attracting abundance, not falling for the scarcity mind trick. It's about going after what truly aligns with who you are and what makes you happy. And what truly makes you happy in the end is never what you end up "owning.

In fact, you never own anything. Sooner or later that thing you grabbed in a moment of urgency will be obsolete or broken a year later.

#7 - The "What You Need" vs. "What You Want" Trap

SOS thrives on "more, more, more!" whether you really need more of something or not.

When you operate from SOS, you lose the distinction between what you need and what you want - you feel like you need everything. You just have to have everything. For example, do you need a pair of socks? Yes, you do. Do you need a few pairs?

Yes, you do. Do you need the latest pair of avocado print socks when you just got the latest pair of sushi print socks? Probably not - you want them, not need them.

Have you ever heard of the Diderot Effect? It comes from the story of the French philosopher Diderot, author of one of the most comprehensive encyclopedias of his time. Though highly respected, he could not afford his daughter's dowry - so Catherine the Great, hearing of his plight, offered to buy his library. The man suddenly found himself with more wealth than he had ever imagined.

At first, he simply acquired a beautiful new scarlet robe. But that was just the beginning. Compared to his new robe, the rest of his possessions seemed out of place, so he got a new Damascus rug. Next came some fine sculptures. And a new kitchen table. A new mirror. A new leather chair to replace his straw one. And on and on came a series of reactive purchases of things he never really needed; he just needed to pay his daughter's dowry.

That's the **Diderot Effect** - one new shiny object followed by another and another, in a spiral of consumption of things you suddenly want but don't really need to feel fulfilled.

If you're really honest, you'll realize that you often buy things you don't need. If you have a shiny new car, you may want to upgrade the wheels or the upholstery or the navigation system - none of which you would have needed with your old car. If you don't have a clear sense of what you really value, the Diderot effect can easily take over.

Why do you keep buying things you don't need? There could be many reasons. Perhaps buying things gives you the pleasure of distraction; it could be a means of escaping boredom. Maybe having a lot of stuff gives you a sense of security. Maybe you think "more" will make you happy. Maybe you're trying to keep up with or surpass someone else. Maybe you buy things out of guilt. Maybe you're just selfish or greedy.

The stream of shiny objects never ends - it's up to you to decide what's valuable to you and what's not. If you find value in something, by all means pursue it. But every once in a while, remind yourself that in many cases less is more. Less is more because instead of "having it all," you will have what really matters. You want to buy what aligns with your values, not what fits into a spiral of unnecessary consumption.

#8 - Believe you are what others say you are

A lot of chasing shiny objects and being afflicted with SOS is about wanting to impress people. You care about what others think of you. You may even believe that you are what others say you are.

When your identity is based solely on other people's perceptions, you will do almost anything to keep them thinking highly of you and to maintain your sense of pride. Combine that with constant advertising - and you've got an SOS cycle that's hard to break out of.

Getting out of this SOS feeding trap is again about maintaining a strong set of beliefs about yourself and what brings you fulfillment in life.

#9 - Not Questioning Hidden Motives

Do you know what the real purpose of social media is? Think about it. What do you tell yourself when you use apps like Instagram or Facebook? Probably that it's a great way to discover new things. Or to stay in touch with old friends. Or to find inspiring content from your favorite coaches. Or to find reviews of something you're thinking about buying.

All of those are true-and they're great reasons. But none of them reflect the primary purpose of social media, which is to sell you something.

If you're aware of the true motives of the tools you use, you'll be less of a target. You'll do things because you want to, not because you're being pushed.

It's great if you want to use Instagram to chat with your friends - but recognize that's why you're on it; so the next time you see that new shiny thing that's trending on Instagram popping up in a store in your feed (which will be soon), you won't let it trigger your impulse to respond.

Next, let's move into the next section where you will go deeper into the four mindset traps of Shiny Object Syndrome...and how to break free of these traps.

Mindset Trap #1:
The Sunk Cost Fallacy

In Henry IV, Shakespeare's Falstaff says, "The better part of valor is discretion."

Overcoming the Sunk Cost Fallacy is essential to improving decision making. This cognitive bias leads you to persistently investing time, money, or effort in a failing venture because of the resources already expended.

It leads to poor decisions and unnecessary losses by clouding judgment with past investments rather than future potential.

Recognizing this fallacy allows people to make more rational decisions, ultimately leading to better opportunities and more satisfying outcomes.

Understanding the Sunk Cost Fallacy

The sunk cost fallacy is a cognitive bias that affects our decision-making processes. At its core, this fallacy occurs when you continue an endeavor simply because you have already invested significant resources such as time, money, or effort in it.

This can lead to irrational decisions in which the primary motivation for persisting is not future benefits or potential success, but rather the desire not to waste what has already been spent.

The roots of this behavior lie in human nature, where past investments weigh heavily on your mind and influence your present decisions. People often cling to past investments in the hope that further effort will eventually lead to success.

For example, consider a business owner who has invested months of work and thousands of dollars in a failing project. Despite continued losses, the owner may persist in pouring more resources into the project, believing that abandoning it would be an admission of wasted time and money.

This situation captures the essence of the Sunk Cost Fallacy, where the focus shifts from making rational, forward-looking decisions to justifying past expenditures.

Eating habits also illustrate the influence of the sunk cost fallacy. People often force themselves to finish meals they've paid for, even when they're full, in order to avoid wasting money. This tendency stems from a desire to make the most of what they've spent, ignoring physical signals of satiety.

This behavior can lead to overeating and health problems in the long run. The discomfort and potential weight gain are clear indications that continuing to eat based solely on the investment made is counterproductive.

Recognizing the Sunk Cost Fallacy is critical to breaking free from its grip and making more rational decisions. When you become aware of this bias, you can begin to evaluate your decisions based on current realities and future prospects rather than past expenditures.

One more example is a student who realizes that she dislikes her chosen field of study and may decide to change her major, even though she has spent years pursuing her original path. By recognizing the sunk cost fallacy, the student can make a choice that better aligns with his or her interests and long-term goals, ultimately leading to greater satisfaction and success.

So, why do we continue to invest in bad investments?

One of the primary psychological reasons for this behavior is the experience of **regret**. Regret occurs when people look back on their decisions and wish they had chosen differently; it drives them to double down on their past choices in an attempt to turn things around and validate their original decisions.

This phenomenon is particularly powerful because the fear of admitting that a past decision was wrong can be overwhelming. By continuing to invest time, money, or resources in a failed endeavor, individuals hope to avoid the emotional discomfort associated with regret.

Moreover, the emotions associated with regret are not limited to feelings of personal failure. Individuals often worry about how others will perceive them. Admitting a mistake publicly can be seen as an admission of poor judgment, which can be damaging to one's self-esteem and social standing.

To avoid these negative emotions, people may persist in trying to make something work, even when the rational choice would be to abandon it. In essence, the desire to avoid regret leads to greater emotional and financial investment in the very decision that needs to be reevaluated (Chu, W., n.d.).

Another powerful factor in the persistence of bad investments is **loss aversion**. Humans are inherently wired to feel the pain of loss more acutely than the pleasure of gain. This bias means that the potential to lose what has already been invested weighs heavily on decision-making processes.

For example, an entrepreneur may continue to pour money into a failing project because he or she believes that pulling out now would mean that all previous investments were for naught. The fear of realizing these losses can lead to irrational behavior, such as refusing to cut one's losses in the hope that the situation will improve.

In many cases, this loss aversion can be so strong that it overrides logical analysis of the situation. A person may see clear evidence that an investment is unlikely to yield positive returns, but still choose to hold on to it because they are emotionally focused on avoiding the loss of their existing investment.

This behavior is often counterproductive, exacerbating the initial loss by wasting additional resources in a futile attempt to salvage the situation. Therefore, understanding and addressing loss aversion is essential to making better, more rational decisions.

Ego and pride also play a significant role in why individuals persist in bad investments. Admitting to oneself and others that a decision was a mistake can be incredibly difficult. Ego drives people to maintain a narrative in which they are competent and always make the right decisions.

When faced with the reality of a bad investment, allowing one's pride to guide decision-making can lead to more bad decisions. Instead of cutting their losses and moving on, individuals may continue to invest in order to maintain their self-image.

In addition, the social dimension of the ego cannot be underestimated. People often involve their social circle in their investment decisions. Admitting failure could mean losing face with peers, family, or colleagues.

This social pressure forces individuals to continue with failing investments rather than admit defeat. The need to maintain a positive self-identity and public image thus becomes a barrier to rational decision-making, trapping individuals in a cycle of poor investments.

Optimism bias is another psychological factor that fuels persistence in losing activities. This bias causes individuals to overestimate the likelihood of future success while underestimating potential risks. Despite repeated failures, optimism bias leads people to believe that success is just around the corner.

Entrepreneurs, gamblers, and everyday investors alike can fall prey to this illusion, convincing themselves that their next investment will be the breakthrough they have been waiting for.

This belief in a rosy future often blinds people to the reality of their current situation. They may ignore clear warning signs and data suggesting that their efforts are failing, instead focusing on hypothetical future successes.

The optimism bias creates false hope and encourages continued investment in projects that are doomed to fail, ultimately resulting in greater losses.

Strategies for Overcoming the Sunk Cost Fallacy

To overcome the sunk cost fallacy, you must first periodically evaluate whether your goals are still worth the continued effort and resources. This involves **critically evaluating all ongoing projects** to determine if they are still aligned with long-term goals and delivering tangible benefits.

Reflecting on your current efforts and identifying those that may no longer be worth your investment can help you make informed decisions about where to allocate your time and energy. For example, a business project that shows no signs of profitability after several years, despite the significant investment already made, may need to be terminated.

Setting measurable milestones is a critical step in effectively monitoring progress. By defining small, measurable milestones for your major goals, you create clear checkpoints that help you measure success and identify potential problems early. These milestones serve as indicators of progress, allowing for timely adjustments or reassessment of the project's viability.

For example, an entrepreneur might set quarterly sales goals to evaluate the performance of a new product, ensuring that each milestone is met before moving forward.

Tracking resources such as time, money, and energy helps identify areas of waste. Start by tracking your daily expenses and time to identify inefficiencies and reduce unnecessary spending.

This practice allows you to allocate resources more wisely, ensuring that they are directed to projects that promise the best return. For example, maintaining a detailed log of project expenses and time spent can reveal hidden costs and productivity lags, allowing you to make necessary course corrections.

Another strategy to combat the sunk cost fallacy is to make decisions based on objective data and facts rather than emotion. Before deciding, list the factual pros and cons to ensure a rational approach.

Emotions often cloud judgment and lead to persistence in failing endeavors. By removing yourself emotionally from the decision-making process, you can analyze situations from a third-person perspective, which facilitates unbiased judgments. This method is especially important in high-stakes environments, where emotional biases can lead to significant misallocation of resources.

By understanding and overcoming the sunk cost fallacy, you can make more rational decisions, avoid unnecessary losses, and open yourself up to better opportunities. Use these strategies to strengthen your decision-making and achieve your goals more effectively.

Understanding and overcoming the sunk cost fallacy can help you make better decisions, avoid unnecessary losses, and open yourself up to better opportunities.

The examples provided illustrate the pervasiveness of this cognitive bias-from gamblers who chase losses to professionals who cling to unsatisfying careers because of past educational expenses. These scenarios help illustrate the real-world implications of the sunk cost fallacy and offer insight into its detrimental effects on both minor and major life decisions.

As you move forward, consider how the principles discussed in this chapter apply to your own life and work. Think about areas where the sunk cost fallacy may be influencing your decisions.

Are there projects or relationships that no longer serve your best interests but are difficult to let go of because of past investments? Embrace the possibility of change and the potential it holds for better opportunities.

Now let's examine the next mindset that feeds into Shiny Object Syndrome: **FOMO—the Fear of Missing Out.**

Mindset Trap #2—FOMO: The Fear of Missing Out

The fear of missing out (FOMO) permeates every aspect of our lives these days.

True success and lasting happiness can only come from focusing on our own individual paths, yet we can't help but look around, compare, or wonder if there's something "better" out there.

Today, those prone to SOS are also easily susceptible to the pitfalls of FOMO. Those who already find themselves chasing shiny objects, if encouraged by the effects of FOMO, will continue to do so, hoping that their "chasing" will reduce their insecurity or sense of lack. Now, it's easier than ever to stay trapped in SOS. After all, there's always something shiny we're missing out on because of what we've chosen to do or have, and there are always countless options and wild rabbits we've said "no" to because we've said "yes" to chasing one more.

Shiny object syndrome thrives on indecision. What happens when all options or objects look equally attractive? What happens when you can't decide? What happens when you don't want to miss anything and you want to have tried every option? You decide to chase one shiny object, then the next, then the next - and so on, in a state of never-ending SOS and FOMO.

Most definitions of FOMO describe it as an "unpleasant emotional reaction. It's about feeling like you're both "missing out" and "left out." When you scroll through Instagram and see beautiful photos of your friend sailing in Greece while you're stuck at your desk, you feel like you're missing out.

When you see the lives and accomplishments of others, you feel inadequate in comparison. You want to have better, do better, be better. At the very least, you want to be their equal. You need validation through social comparison, and when that doesn't happen, your self-worth takes a hit. And so, it becomes easy to fall into the trap of chasing shiny objects, thinking they will help us feel or look "better.

Breaking the FOMO Cycle

Overcoming FOMO (the Fear of Missing Out) can lead to a more balanced and fulfilling life. The fear of not being present at every event or missing out on important experiences can cause unnecessary stress and anxiety. By shifting the focus from constant involvement in every activity to recognizing which moments truly align with personal goals and values, you can find peace in your choices.

Considering alternative ways to get information or stay current without feeling the need to attend every meeting or social gathering is emphasized. By recognizing the effort behind success and understanding that achievements often involve invisible struggles, you can mitigate feelings of envy and FOMO. This shift from jealousy to appreciation fosters a more positive outlook and encourages empathy for others' journeys.

Engaging in solo activities and finding happiness in solitude can reduce reliance on social validation and increase self-awareness. This not only builds confidence, but also promotes resilience to external pressures.

Now, here are six strategies I personally engage with to keep my FOMO moments at a minimum, while adding to my personal growth journey.

Six Ways to Break the FOMO Pattern

Strategy 1: Accept Imperfection

An effective strategy for overcoming FOMO is to **accept imperfection.** When you understand that missing an event or moment isn't the end of the world, you begin to see life from a more balanced perspective.

Consider the worst-case scenario. Imagining the worst possible outcome of missing an event can be quite enlightening. Often, the situations we exaggerate in our minds turn out to be far less serious when we examine them closely.

For example, if you skip a party, the worst that can happen is that you miss a social interaction or a bit of gossip. But this loss usually doesn't affect your long-term happiness or success. By addressing and confronting these exaggerated fears, we can see that the fear of missing out is often unfounded.

Recognizing non-catastrophic outcomes is another important step. It's important to realize that missing an event does not drastically affect your value or success. For example, missing a seminar doesn't mean you're behind in your career. There are always opportunities to catch up, learn and grow.

We often place too much emphasis on single events, forgetting that life is a series of continuous learning experiences. Embracing this understanding helps reduce FOMO and promotes mental well-being by reducing unnecessary stress and anxiety.

Embrace limited participation by acknowledging that you don't have to be a part of everything to feel validated. In today's hyper-connected world, there's a misconception that constant participation equals value.

But being selective about where and how you invest your time can lead to more meaningful experiences. It's about quality over quantity - deeper, more fulfilling interactions come from genuine interest, not a compulsion to be everywhere. This realization empowers you to make choices that align with your true interests and values, further reducing feelings of FOMO.

To put this into practice, one actionable step is to **write down the worst-case scenario** the next time you feel FOMO creeping in. Think about why it's not as bad as it seems. This process not only provides clarity, but also helps to reframe your mindset.

Documenting your thoughts can reveal patterns in your thinking that exaggerate the importance of certain events. Over time, this exercise can train your brain to take a more balanced view, reducing the grip that FOMO has on you. It also reduces the risk of chasing after shiny objects. This can be as simple as jotting down your fears in a notebook or using a dedicated app on your phone.

Once documented, analyze and reflect on each scenario. Consider alternative perspectives and realistic outcomes. Over time, this practice can build mental resilience, allowing you to face FOMO with a more balanced and calmer mindset.

Strategy 2: Enjoying Solitude

Finding happiness on your own reduces the need for social validation and creates a more balanced and fulfilling life.

One effective way to do this is to regularly engage in solitary activities. These can range from reading a compelling book to exploring nature through hiking. When you engage in these activities alone, you have the opportunity to discover what truly brings you joy without the influence or expectations of others. For example, hiking allows you to connect with nature, reflect, and enjoy solitude, all of which contribute to inner peace and happiness.

Solo activities also give you the opportunity to delve deeply into your interests. Without the distractions or interruptions that often come with social interactions, you can experience a deeper engagement with your chosen activity.

Whether it's getting lost in a gripping novel, or concentrating intensely on painting, the quality of the experience is enhanced when you're alone. This deep immersion not only increases enjoyment, but also promotes personal growth as you develop a stronger connection to your passions and hobbies.

To reinforce this newfound independence and self-reliance, it is important to take actionable steps. One practical way to start is to **actively schedule time each week** for a solo activity. This could include setting aside an hour to read a book, take a walk in the park, or engage in a hobby that you enjoy by yourself.

By prioritizing these moments, you create a routine that allows you to reconnect with yourself and your interests on a regular basis. Over time, this practice becomes habitual, and the benefits of reduced social dependency and increased personal happiness become more pronounced.

Self-reflection is critical to personal development because it helps you understand yourself better and make decisions that align with your values and desires. For example, **journaling during your alone** time can provide insight into your innermost thoughts and feelings, which can help build self-awareness and emotional intelligence.

Strategy 3: Build an Offline Existence

Reducing digital dependence increases real-world connections, which has profound benefits for individuals seeking a balanced life. Our reliance on social media often takes a toll on our ability to fully engage with the people and activities around us. By intentionally unplugging from social media, you can reclaim time and focus that might otherwise be fragmented by constant notifications and online distractions.

Instead of scrolling through feeds, people can engage in offline activities like playing board games with friends or enjoying family dinners without digital interruptions. This helps strengthen personal relationships and create lasting memories rooted in real-life experiences rather than virtual interactions.

When we step away from digital screens and participate in face-to-face interactions, we open ourselves up to new perspectives and fresh insights.

Offline interactions allow us to immerse ourselves in conversations without the constraints of character limits or the pressure to curate the perfect post. Engaging in discussions on a hike, at a coffee shop, or even at a local community event can rejuvenate our minds and expose us to different points of view.

These interactions often provide a sense of fulfillment and connection that digital exchanges can't replicate. According to Anderson et al. (2018), while digital technology has its benefits, it is important to balance it with real-world engagement to maintain holistic well-being.

Emotional freedom is another important benefit of reducing digital dependency. Digital interruptions can fragment our attention spans and increase stress levels, leading to a less fulfilling emotional life. By setting limits on digital use and focusing on offline activities, individuals can enjoy moments of peace and mental clarity.

The absence of constant alerts and notifications allows for deeper emotional engagement with the present moment. This emotional freedom leads to reduced anxiety and a greater ability to face life's challenges with a clear mind. It also fosters authentic relationships, as conversations become more meaningful when there is undivided attention.

Engaging in offline activities on a regular basis can be transformative. It's not just about taking a break from screens, it's about enriching your life with tangible experiences. These activities can range from taking up a new hobby, attending a live concert, joining a sports team, or simply having deep conversations with loved ones.

Each of these offline engagements brings unique rewards that contribute to personal growth and relationship depth. They encourage us to develop skills, create art, build physical stamina, and nurture bonds, all of which contribute to a more balanced and fulfilling life.

New perspectives are essential to personal growth. When we limit our interactions to digital spaces, we miss out on the spontaneous, unfiltered experiences that physical interactions provide. Conversations during a leisurely walk or group fitness class can inspire creative thoughts and solutions that we might not stumble upon in the digital realm.

Real-life interactions are raw and authentic, offering a refreshing change from the often polished and edited narratives we encounter online. These experiences fuel our creativity and empathy, making us better equipped to navigate life's complexities.

Strategy 4: Identify Your FOMO Triggers

Identifying triggers for FOMO is an essential step in managing how we respond to these feelings. One of the most effective ways to do this is by **journaling instances of FOMO**. Keeping a journal helps you become more aware of specific moments when FOMO occurs.

For example, note the time of day, what you were doing, and what specifically triggered the feeling. Was it a social media post, a conversation with friends, or perhaps seeing an event you weren't invited to? By documenting these details, patterns may emerge that provide insight into common triggers.

Reflecting on whether these feelings are externally influenced or internally conditioned is the next important step. It's important to distinguish whether FOMO is caused by external factors, such as peer pressure and societal expectations, or whether it's more about internal conditioning, such as personal insecurities and desires.

Seeing others enjoying a vacation may trigger FOMO due to societal standards of success and leisure. On the other hand, FOMO can also come from self-imposed pressures, such as believing that you must attend every social event to feel validated.

Understanding these differences can help you better analyze and manage your reactions. Are your reactions driven by a genuine desire for connection and experience, or are they fueled by an urge to fulfill perceived social obligations?

This awareness allows you to question the validity of your feelings and choose healthier responses. Instead of succumbing to impulsive behaviors like mindlessly scrolling through social media, you can choose more fulfilling activities that align with your true interests and values.

By journaling for a week and analyzing your FOMO triggers, you can create a practical framework for understanding and addressing these feelings.

Reflect on each entry: What caused the feeling of missing out, and how did you respond? Consider alternative ways you could have handled the situation.

Over time, this practice not only helps you identify patterns, but also provides an opportunity to develop coping mechanisms tailored to your unique triggers.

In essence, you're training your mind to process these moments constructively, building resilience against future episodes of FOMO.

Strategy 5: Reinforcing Positive Thinking and Experiences

When we shift our focus to positivity, it can remarkably transform our mindset. This shift begins by reframing negativity. Often, negative thoughts creep into our minds unnoticed and color our perceptions and actions. By actively catching these thoughts and reframing them positively, we begin to change the way we view challenges and setbacks.

For example, instead of thinking, "I failed at this task," we can say, "I learned a lot from this experience. This simple shift in language can gradually build a more positive outlook. It's about training the mind to see opportunities for growth rather than just obstacles.

Transforming feelings of envy into joy is another powerful way to cultivate positivity. Envy can be a destructive emotion, making us feel inadequate and resentful. But by recognizing others' accomplishments as sources of inspiration rather than threats, we open ourselves up to appreciation and joy.

When a colleague is promoted, celebrating their success can boost our own morale and motivate us to strive for greater heights. This practice helps develop an abundance mindset, where there's enough success for everyone and someone else's gain is not seen as our loss.

Focusing on the good aspects of life significantly changes our overall perspective. It's easy to dwell on what went wrong or what's missing, but intentionally focusing on the positive can make a profound difference in how we experience life. Every day has its struggles, but in the midst of them are moments of joy, accomplishment, and kindness.

By anchoring our attention on these positives, we reduce the weight of negative experiences. This doesn't mean we ignore problems; rather, it's a matter of balancing our perspective and ensuring that the good doesn't overshadow the bad. This balanced perspective fosters resilience and a more optimistic outlook on life.

As an actionable step to reinforce this shift toward positivity, it's beneficial to adopt the habit of daily reflection on positive events. Each day, take a few minutes to **write down three positive things** that have happened. These could be personal accomplishments, kind interactions, or even simple pleasures like enjoying a good meal.

This practice, recommended by many psychologists, serves as a tangible reminder of the good in our lives. It also trains the brain to seek out and appreciate positive experiences, gradually creating a more positive default state of mind.

Strategy 6: Simplify Trivial Decisions

Simplifying decisions conserves mental energy and allows us to live a more productive and focused life. Daily life presents us with numerous choices, from what to wear to what to eat. By simplifying these routine decisions, we can reduce some of the cognitive load that hinders our efficiency.

One effective way to make everyday decisions easier is to simplify your wardrobe choices. For example, choosing a few versatile outfits reduces the time spent each morning deciding what to wear.

Many successful people, such as Steve Jobs or Mark Zuckerberg, are known for their minimalist approach to clothing, usually sticking to a simple uniform. This not only reduces the amount of decision making, but also ensures that you start your day with less stress.

A similar approach can be applied to **meal planning**; deciding on weekly menus in advance eliminates the need to think about daily meal choices. Preparing and freezing meals over the weekend can free up significant mental space during the week.

Freeing up mental space by simplifying routine decisions allows you to redirect cognitive energy to more critical tasks. When we're not overloaded with trivial choices, our minds are clearer and better able to handle complex problems. Decision fatigue, the deterioration of decision quality after a long period of decision making, can severely impact our personal and professional lives.

By reducing the number of inconsequential decisions, we reserve our mental resources for things that really matter, such as strategic planning at work or meaningful interactions with loved ones. Simplifying decisions, such as choosing what to wear or planning meals, creates room for creativity and innovation by reducing the constant mental chatter that slows us down.

Decision fatigue is a common problem that many of us face. Each decision we make consumes a bit of our finite supply of mental energy. The concept, identified by social psychologist Dr. Roy Baumeister, states that after making numerous decisions, we become less and less capable of making sound choices.

This can manifest as procrastination, impulsivity, indecision, or avoidance. To combat this, simplification strategies play a critical role in minimizing decision fatigue. Limiting the number of choices in our daily lives - such as what to wear, what to eat, or what to do with our free time - can reduce the extent of this fatigue and improve overall mental well-being.

An actionable step to see the benefits firsthand is to simplify one daily decision for an entire week. Start small by focusing on one aspect, such as your breakfast routine. Decide ahead of time what you're going to eat each morning for a week, whether it's oatmeal, smoothies, or scrambled eggs.

Make this small change and see how much mental ease it brings to your mornings. Observe the increase in focus and productivity throughout the day, then consider expanding this practice to other areas of your life. Over time, as simplified decision-making becomes a habit, you'll notice a significant improvement in your ability to handle more important matters without feeling overwhelmed.

Simplifying everyday decisions not only conserves mental energy, but also prepares you mentally for more significant challenges. Simplified routines create consistency and reliability, which are essential for maintaining mental stability.

For example, laying out your clothes the night before or having a preset menu for weeknight dinner simplifies your evening routine and frees you from unnecessary stress. This leaves you better equipped to deal with unexpected events or emergencies as they arise. As a result, adopting these habits will benefit both your mental health and your performance in various aspects of your life.

In conclusion

By adopting these strategies, you can overcome the fear of missing out and live a more balanced, fulfilling life. The consequences of implementing these practices extend beyond personal well-being, positively impacting professional productivity and interpersonal relationships.

As we continue to navigate an increasingly interconnected world, it will become increasingly important to stay grounded in our values and focused on what really matters.

Mindset Trap #3—The Fear of Better Options (FOBO)

Fear of Better Options (FOBO) is the fear that arises when we're faced with too many choices, which can lead to indecision and inaction. FOBO is closely related to Shiny Object Syndrome, as both can cause us to become distracted and lose sight of our long-term goals.

FOBO can occur when we're presented with too many options, each of which seems better than the last. With so many appealing choices, it's easy to feel overwhelmed and indecisive, leading us to procrastinate or not decide at all.

When it comes to Shiny Object Syndrome, FOBO can be a major contributing factor. We may feel that we need to pursue every new idea or opportunity that comes our way, lest we miss out on something better.

This fear of missing out can cause us to lose sight of our current goals and priorities and get sidetracked by shiny objects that don't ultimately serve us.

To combat FOBO and Shiny Object Syndrome, it's important to clarify our goals and priorities so we know what we're working toward. By having a clear vision of what we want to achieve, we can better evaluate new opportunities and ideas as they arise and decide which ones will help us get closer to our goals.

The FOBO Solution

Imagine a busy professional who is constantly bombarded with new job opportunities. With each new option, the fear of making the wrong choice increases, leading to indecision and procrastination.

Similarly, an entrepreneur may find himself distracted by the latest business trend and unable to focus on his primary goals due to the lure of potentially "better" opportunities. Students can also suffer from these problems, jumping from one learning method to another without sticking with one long enough to see results. These examples illustrate how FOBO and Shiny Object Syndrome create a cycle of distraction and inaction that prevents individuals from making consistent progress in their pursuits.

Break your "FOBO" action plan

It's important to recognize how FOBO and Shiny Object Syndrome influence each other. When we're constantly bombarded with new possibilities, it becomes difficult to commit to a single path. Our attention shifts, making it difficult to achieve sustained focus and productivity. This cycle fuels further anxiety, exacerbating both conditions.

By understanding these connections, we can better address the root cause: the relentless drive to make optimal choices. In a world full of distractions, it's critical to cultivate mindfulness and intentionality in our decision-making processes. This means being aware of your triggers - those moments when new options seem irresistibly appealing - and taking deliberate steps to refocus on your primary goals.

Focus on small steps: Instead of analyzing every potential decision to death, start with manageable, smaller decisions. This can help build momentum and confidence in your decision-making process.

Embrace imperfection: Understand that not every decision will be perfect. Learning to accept this can reduce the pressure we put on ourselves and reduce the anxiety associated with making decisions.

Set deadlines: By setting deadlines for decisions, you can break through the paralysis of over-analysis. Deadlines force action and limit the endless pursuit of the "perfect" option.

Prioritize ruthlessly: Identify what really matters in your personal and professional life. By distinguishing between urgent and important tasks, you can allocate your time and energy more effectively.

Consult trusted sources: Sometimes seeking advice from mentors or peers can provide clarity. They may be able to offer perspectives that simplify the decision-making process and keep you from getting sidetracked.

Another technique is to develop a **reflective practice**. Regularly evaluating your goals and progress allows you to adjust without feeling overwhelmed by endless choices. Reflective practices such as journaling or weekly reviews create space to reevaluate priorities and ensure alignment with long-term goals.

The anxiety caused by FOBO and its relationship to shiny object syndrome are significant barriers to effective decision-making and long-term goal achievement.

By implementing thoughtful strategies and fostering an environment conducive to focus, individuals can overcome the challenges posed by these modern-day afflictions. Taking conscious steps to prioritize, set boundaries, and reflect regularly can help alleviate these anxieties and promote a more balanced, productive life.

Reflect on current goals: Take time periodically to review what you are currently working on and why those tasks are important. This reflection helps reinforce your commitment to these projects and reduces the temptation to abandon them for something new.

Set clear criteria for new opportunities: Before jumping into a new project, evaluate whether it aligns with your long-term goals. Ask yourself if the new idea will really benefit you more than what you're already doing.

Create a decision framework: Design a system that includes specific criteria for evaluating opportunities. This might include considering the potential return on investment, alignment with your goals, and effort required.

Limit exposure to distractions: Reduce the number of opportunities you are exposed to at any given time. This could mean limiting the amount of time you spend surfing the Internet or attending fewer networking events.

By incorporating these strategies, it's possible to minimize the effects of FOBO and Shiny Object Syndrome. Not only will these methods help you make better decisions, they'll also increase your productivity and give you a sense of control over your choices.

More broadly, fostering an environment that supports focused work and minimizes unnecessary interruptions can significantly improve productivity and well-being. A cultural shift toward valuing deep work and sustained attention can propel organizations and individuals to greater heights. The rest of this book focuses on creating a plan for deeper focus and a clearer mindset that is designed to combat shiny objects.

Remember that managing these fears requires conscious action and reflection. By incorporating thoughtful strategies into our routines, we can navigate the many choices of the modern world with clarity and purpose. In doing so, we pave the way for consistent progress and meaningful success.

Mindset Trap #4—Multi-tasking and Shiny Object Syndrome

Multitasking is often considered a hallmark of productivity. Many people believe that managing multiple tasks simultaneously allows them to accomplish more in less time. However, the cognitive demands and mental strain associated with multitasking can have significant drawbacks that impact both productivity and mental health.

When people try to juggle multiple activities at once, their attention becomes fragmented, making it difficult to excel at any one task. This divided focus is not only inefficient, but also detrimental to overall well-being.

Multitasking - An Overview

Multitasking is often thought of as the ability to manage multiple tasks simultaneously, but the reality is more complex. At its core, multitasking is the attempt to perform multiple tasks simultaneously or to switch rapidly between different activities.

The appeal of multitasking lies in the belief that it increases productivity by getting more done in less time. However, understanding what multitasking really entails can help us understand why it often leads to counterproductive results.

One of the fundamental aspects of multitasking is switching between tasks quickly, rather than doing them all at once. When you multitask, your brain engages in a process called "task switching," in which your attention quickly shifts from one task to another. This constant shifting requires the brain to reorient itself each time, resulting in brief cognitive delays known as "switching costs.

These costs manifest themselves in reduced speed and accuracy, increased error rates, and higher cognitive load, making multitasking far less efficient than it may seem.

Multitasking is not limited to professional environments; it permeates our daily personal activities as well. At work, employees may juggle emails, reports, and phone calls at the same time, mistaking it for increased efficiency. At home, individuals may cook dinner while answering texts and supervising children's homework. Despite the prevalence and seeming necessity of multitasking in modern life, research consistently shows that the practice does more harm than good.

A common misconception is that multitasking is a valuable skill. However, scientific studies have shown that frequent multitaskers often perform worse on various cognitive tasks than those who focus on one task at a time.

For example, high-media multitaskers tend to score lower on attention and memory tests than low-media multitaskers. Overestimating their ability to process multiple streams of information simultaneously often leads to subpar performance, challenging the notion that multitasking is a desirable skill.

Attempting to perform multiple tasks in rapid succession consumes significant mental resources, which can lead to cognitive overload. This phenomenon becomes particularly clear when one examines the brain's neurological response to multitasking.

Brain imaging studies have shown that key areas responsible for executive control and sustained attention are heavily taxed during multitasking, struggling to allocate attention efficiently among competing tasks. As a result, the deeper and more complex processing required for high-level tasks is compromised.

Multitasking is Not Just for the Office

Daily personal activities are not immune to the detrimental effects of multitasking. Whether it's driving while talking on the phone, watching TV while texting, or eating while working on a laptop, these behaviors can lead to inattention and accidents. The effects of distracted driving alone illustrate how multitasking can pose serious safety risks. In addition, divided attention diminishes the enjoyment and mindfulness of everyday experiences, ultimately reducing overall well-being.

The myth of multitasking as a productivity enhancer overlooks the intricate complexity of human cognition. Our brains are not designed to handle multiple tasks with equal efficiency, and forcing them to do so only leads to diminished performance and increased stress.

Studies have shown that even seemingly automated tasks, such as walking and chewing gum, require some level of cognitive input. When more complex tasks are introduced into the mix, the cognitive demand increases exponentially. This is because each task competes for limited mental resources, creating a bottleneck effect that slows task completion and amplifies errors. Thus, while the intent behind multitasking may be to maximize productivity, the result is often the opposite.

The Cost of Task Switching

Frequent task switching significantly reduces efficiency due to the cognitive costs associated with switching between tasks.

These switching costs arise because each shift requires cognitive effort to reorient, reassess, and reallocate attention. This process is not instantaneous; it takes time for the brain to adjust, resulting in inefficiency.

Frequent task switching also leads to mental fatigue, which reduces overall productivity. Mental fatigue results from the constant demand on cognitive resources to repeatedly shift focus. The brain's executive control functions are heavily taxed during this process, leading to a more rapid onset of fatigue.

Managing multiple tasks often requires significant cognitive effort to manage different sets of rules, goals, and information streams. This overload not only fatigues the mind, but also impairs decision-making and critical thinking skills.

A fatigued mind finds it difficult to effectively prioritize tasks and make sound judgments, leading to impaired performance in all activities. In the long run, this can lead to chronic mental fatigue, which can cause burnout and affect overall well-being.

Embrace focused work

By defining multitasking and revealing the process of task switching, we have shown how frequent shifts of attention lead to cognitive overload and inefficiency. The revelations about the brain's limitations in managing multiple tasks simultaneously brought clarity to why multitasking often leads to poorer outcomes rather than greater productivity.

Returning to Shiny Object Syndrome (SOS), we see a clear link between the lure of new tasks and the fragmentation of focus. The tendency to chase new, appealing opportunities instead of completing current tasks is an example of how divided attention can derail progress.

As we look to the future, it is imperative that we embrace focused attention and mindful work habits. Recognizing the limits of our cognitive abilities allows us to make conscious choices about how we manage our tasks. By choosing depth over breadth and prioritizing individual tasks, we can improve our productivity, reduce stress, and foster a healthier work environment.

The 'Trimmed Blueprint' to Solve Multitasking

As we know, multitasking leads to fragmented attention, reduced productivity, increased error rates, cognitive overload, and mental fatigue. It also contributes to the tendency to chase new and exciting tasks instead of completing current ones, resulting in numerous unfinished projects and feelings of inadequacy and burnout.

Now, I'll present you with a detailed blueprint that you can use to significantly reduce the multi-tasking habit. Review this plan every morning before you start your day, and stay focused on eliminating the pursuit of Shiny Objects.

Here are three stages of removing multi-tasking as one of the barriers to becoming your greater self

Step 1: Implement Single-tasking and Task Prioritization

Single-tasking: Focus on One Task at a Time

Objective: Enhance concentration and productivity by dedicating your attention to one task at a time.

1. Focus on One Task at a Time:

- **Eliminate Distractions:** Before starting a task, create an environment conducive to focus. Close unnecessary tabs on your browser, silence your phone, and inform colleagues or family members of your focused work time.
- **Set Clear Intentions:** Begin each task with a clear understanding of what you want to achieve. Write down your objective for the task to keep your focus aligned.

- **Commit Fully:** Dedicate your full attention to the task at hand. Avoid switching to other tasks or checking notifications until you have completed your focused work session.

2. Break Down Larger Tasks into Smaller, Manageable Chunks:

- **Identify the Components:** Take a large task and break it down into smaller, more manageable steps. For example, if your task is to write a report, break it down into researching, outlining, writing the introduction, and so on.
- **Create a Checklist:** List these smaller tasks as a checklist. This will give you a clear pathway and provide a sense of accomplishment as you check off each item.
- **Set Time Limits:** Assign specific time limits to each small task to ensure you stay on track and maintain momentum.

3. Use Tools like the Pomodoro Technique:

- **25-Minute Work Sessions:** Set a timer for 25 minutes and focus solely on one task during this period. This is known as a Pomodoro session.
- **5-Minute Breaks:** After the timer goes off, take a 5-minute break to rest and recharge. Use this time to stretch, grab a drink, or take a short walk.
- **Repeat the Cycle:** Repeat the 25-minute work session and 5-minute break cycle. After four Pomodoros, take a longer break of 15-30 minutes to rest deeply before starting another cycle.

Task Prioritization: Prioritize Tasks Based on Their Importance and Urgency

Objective: Manage your workload effectively by focusing on tasks that matter most.

1. Use the Eisenhower Matrix to Categorize Tasks:

Quadrant 1: Important and Urgent (Do First):

Tasks in this quadrant require immediate attention and have significant consequences if not completed promptly. Examples include critical deadlines, urgent problems, and last-minute requests.

Quadrant 2: Important but Not Urgent (Schedule):

These tasks are important for long-term success but do not require immediate action. Examples include strategic planning, personal development, and relationship building. Schedule specific times to work on these tasks to ensure they receive the attention they deserve.

Quadrant 3: Not Important but Urgent (Delegate):

Tasks that are urgent but not important often involve responding to other people's needs and requests. Examples include certain meetings, interruptions, and minor tasks. Delegate these tasks when possible to free up time for more important work.

Quadrant 4: Not Important and Not Urgent (Eliminate):

Tasks in this quadrant are neither important nor urgent and often serve as distractions. Examples include excessive social media use, watching TV, and unnecessary meetings. Eliminate or minimize these tasks to focus on what truly matters.

2. Focus on Completing Tasks in the Important and Urgent Quadrant First:

Daily Prioritization: At the start of each day, review your task list and identify which tasks fall into the Important and Urgent quadrant. Prioritize these tasks and allocate time to complete them first.

Plan Ahead: Use the end of each day to plan for the next. Review what you accomplished and what remains, and adjust your priorities accordingly to stay on track.

Stay Flexible: While prioritizing tasks, remain flexible to accommodate unexpected important and urgent tasks that may arise. Adapt your schedule as needed, but always return to your prioritized list.

3. Regularly Review and Adjust Your Prioritization:

Weekly Reviews: Conduct a weekly review to assess your progress and re-evaluate your priorities. Adjust your task list and Eisenhower Matrix based on new developments and shifting priorities.

Monthly Goals: Set monthly goals that align with your long-term objectives. Break these goals down into weekly and daily tasks, using the Eisenhower Matrix to keep your focus on what's most important.

Reflect and Learn: Take time to reflect on what worked well and what didn't. Use these insights to improve your task management and prioritization strategies continually.

By implementing single-tasking and task prioritization techniques, you can significantly enhance your productivity and reduce the negative impacts of multitasking. This action blueprint provides a clear and actionable framework to help you stay focused, manage your time effectively, and achieve your goals with greater efficiency and satisfaction.

Step 2: Identify Personal Multitasking Triggers

To effectively combat the negative effects of multitasking, it's crucial to understand your personal multitasking habits and triggers. By identifying these triggers, you can develop strategies to manage them and improve your focus and productivity.

Conduct a Self-Assessment

Objective: Recognize your personal multitasking habits and identify the triggers that lead you to switch tasks frequently.

1. Reflect on Your Current Habits:

- Take a few minutes to think about your typical workday. When do you find yourself switching between tasks the most?
- Consider both professional and personal contexts. Do you tend to multitask more at work or at home?
- Reflect on the types of tasks you commonly try to juggle simultaneously. Are they related, or do they span different areas of your life?

2. Identify Common Triggers:

- External Triggers: These can include notifications from your phone or computer, incoming emails, colleagues or family members interrupting you, or environmental factors like noise.
- Internal Triggers: These are related to your emotions and mental state. For example, feeling bored, anxious, or stressed can prompt you to switch tasks to seek relief or stimulation.

3. Ask Yourself Key Questions:

- When do I feel the urge to switch tasks? Is it during specific times of the day or when performing certain types of tasks?
- What emotions do I experience when I switch tasks? Am I trying to avoid something unpleasant, or am I seeking excitement?

* How often do I complete tasks I start without interruption? Do I frequently leave tasks unfinished to start something new?

Keep a Distraction Diary

Objective: Document instances of multitasking over a week to identify patterns and their impact on productivity and stress levels.

1. Set Up Your Diary:

* Use a notebook, a spreadsheet, or a digital note-taking app to record your observations.
* Create columns for the date, time, task you were working on, what distracted you, and your emotional state at the time.

2. Document Each Instance of Multitasking:

* Whenever you catch yourself switching tasks, note down the details in your diary.
* Record what task you were initially working on and what task you switched to.
* Note any external triggers (e.g., notifications, interruptions) and internal triggers (e.g., boredom, stress) that prompted the switch.
* Reflect on your emotional state before and after switching tasks.

3. Evaluate the Impact:

* At the end of each day, review your entries and reflect on how multitasking affected your productivity and stress levels.
* Did switching tasks help you get more done, or did it lead to incomplete work and increased stress?

- How did you feel at the end of the day? Were you more stressed and exhausted, or did you feel accomplished and productive?

Analyze Your Findings

1. Identify Patterns:

- After a week, review your distraction diary and look for common patterns.
- Are there specific times of the day when you are more prone to multitasking?
- Do certain tasks consistently trigger multitasking behaviors?

2. Recognize Key Triggers:

- Highlight the most frequent external and internal triggers.
- Reflect on how these triggers align with your emotional states and overall productivity.

3. Develop Strategies to Manage Triggers:

- Based on your findings, create a plan to manage your triggers. For example, if notifications are a major trigger, consider turning them off during work hours.
- If internal triggers like boredom or stress are prevalent, explore techniques such as mindfulness, regular breaks, or varying your tasks to maintain engagement.
- By conducting a self-assessment and keeping a distraction diary, you gain valuable insights into your multitasking habits and triggers. This understanding allows you to implement targeted strategies to minimize distractions, enhance focus, and ultimately improve your productivity and well-being.

Step 3: Set Clear Goals and Commit to Completion

Setting clear goals and committing to seeing tasks through to completion are essential steps in overcoming multitasking and Shiny Object Syndrome (SOS).

Clear goals provide direction and purpose, while commitment ensures that you stay focused and follow through on your intentions.

Set Clear Goals

Objective: Define specific, achievable goals for each project or task to provide direction and maintain focus.

1. Define Your Goals:

SMART Goals in 5 steps: Ensure that your goals are Specific, Measurable, Achievable, Relevant, and Time-bound.

1. **Specific:** Clearly define what you want to achieve. Instead of setting a vague goal like "be more productive," specify tasks like "complete the project proposal by Friday."
2. **Measurable:** Determine how you will measure your progress. For example, "write 1,000 words daily" is a measurable goal.
3. **Achievable:** Set realistic goals that challenge you but are attainable. Consider your current workload and resources.
4. **Relevant:** Align your goals with your long-term objectives and priorities. Ensure they contribute to your overall mission.
5. **Time-bound:** Set a deadline for each goal. Having a timeframe creates a sense of urgency and helps prioritize tasks.

2. Write Down Your Goals:

- Physically writing down your goals increases commitment and accountability.
- Keep your goals visible in your workspace. Use sticky notes, a whiteboard, or a digital task manager to display them prominently.

3. Break Down Goals into Actionable Steps:

Divide larger goals into smaller, manageable tasks. This makes them less overwhelming and more achievable.

For example, if your goal is to "launch a new website," break it down into steps like "choose a domain name," "design the homepage," and "write content for the About page."

4. Prioritize Your Goals:

Use prioritization techniques like the Eisenhower Matrix to focus on tasks that are important and urgent.

Regularly review and adjust your priorities based on changing circumstances and progress.

Commit to Completion

Objective: Develop a habit of seeing tasks through to completion before starting new ones, ensuring consistent progress and avoiding the pitfalls of multitasking.

1. Focus on One Task at a Time:

- Practice single-tasking by dedicating your full attention to one task until it is completed.
- Use the Pomodoro Technique to maintain focus: work for 25 minutes on a single task, then take a 5-minute break. Repeat this cycle and take a longer break after four sessions.

2. Use Accountability Tools and Partners:

- **Accountability Tools:** Use apps and tools like Trello, Asana, or Habitica to track your progress and stay organized.
- **Accountability Partners:** Share your goals with a friend, colleague, or mentor who can provide support and hold you accountable. Regular check-ins can help maintain your commitment.

3. Create a Reward System:

- Reinforce positive behavior by rewarding yourself for completing tasks and projects.
- Rewards can be small, such as taking a short break, enjoying a favorite snack, or spending time on a hobby.
- Celebrating your achievements boosts motivation and reinforces the habit of task completion.

4. Reflect and Adjust:

- At the end of each day or week, review your progress. Reflect on what worked well and what could be improved.
- Make necessary adjustments to your strategies and goals based on your reflections.
- Continuously refine your approach to maintain focus and productivity.

Example Goals and Commitment Plan

Goal: Complete the monthly sales report by the end of the week.

Action Steps:

- Gather sales data from all team members by Tuesday.
- Analyze data and create charts by Wednesday.
- Write the report and review it by Thursday.

- Submit the final report by Friday.

Accountability: Share this goal with your manager and set a reminder for each action step.

Reward: Treat yourself to a nice lunch on Friday after submitting the report.

Goal: Launch a new marketing campaign in two weeks.

Action Steps:

- Brainstorm campaign ideas and select the best one by Monday.
- Develop campaign content and visuals by Wednesday.
- Schedule and test the campaign by the following Monday.
- Launch the campaign and monitor its performance.

Accountability: Regularly update your marketing team on progress and set milestones.

Reward: Take a day off to relax and recharge after the campaign launch.

By setting clear, specific goals and committing to their completion, you can effectively combat the negative effects of multitasking and SOS. This approach helps you stay focused, maintain productivity, and achieve your objectives with greater efficiency and satisfaction.

Conclusion

Throughout this chapter, we explored the detrimental effects of multitasking and Shiny Object Syndrome on productivity. Key strategies like breaking down larger tasks into manageable chunks, using the Pomodoro Technique, and implementing the

Eisenhower Matrix were discussed as practical methods to maintain focus and manage time effectively.

Additionally, optimizing both physical and digital environments to minimize distractions and setting clear, specific goals were highlighted as crucial steps toward achieving focused work. Adapting these techniques requires a shift in mindset— understanding that true productivity is not about being constantly busy but about making meaningful progress on important tasks.

In the following section—and preceding chapters—I will share key strategies and prioritization techniques to help you overcome shiny object syndrome, improve your focus, and get crystal clear on your goals for the future.

PART 3:

Prioritization Techniques and the POWER Framework

"It's not always that we need to do more but rather that we need to focus on less."

—*Nathan W. Morris*

Prioritization Techniques and Enhancing Focus

Managing your ever-growing list of daily tasks can feel like juggling a dozen balls in the air. Each task screams for attention, and they pile up until they become unmanageable, leading to stress and decreased productivity.

For busy people, finding effective ways to prioritize these tasks is essential to maintaining both efficiency and sanity. This chapter explores a crucial aspect of productive time management-prioritization techniques-that can help you navigate the chaos and avoid falling into the Shiny Object Syndrome trap.

Consider this: You start your day with a clear plan, but soon find yourself inundated with urgent emails, unexpected meetings, and last-minute requests. By midday, the prioritized tasks that truly contribute to your long-term goals have been sacrificed on the altar of urgency. This scenario is all too common and illustrates the core problem many face - distinguishing between what's really important and what appears to be.

The distinction between urgent and important tasks is often blurred, resulting in a reactive rather than proactive approach to work. Urgent tasks tend to overshadow important tasks, causing you to focus on short-term fixes at the expense of meaningful progress toward larger goals.

Next, I'll introduce tools such as the Eisenhower Matrix, which categorizes tasks to help you make more informed decisions about where to focus your efforts. We will also discuss strategies for breaking down complex projects into manageable steps and implementing time-blocking methods to increase productivity.

By applying these techniques, you can transform the way you manage your day-to-day responsibilities, allowing you to focus on the activities that really matter and move you toward your long-term goals.

The Eisenhower Matrix (for deep prioritization)

A widely recommended tool for effectively prioritizing tasks is the Eisenhower Matrix. Developed by former U.S. President Dwight D. Eisenhower, this method divides tasks into four distinct categories based on their urgency and importance. It allows individuals to focus on actions that truly contribute to their goals.

The Eisenhower Matrix divides tasks into four quadrants: Urgent and Important, Important but Not Urgent, Urgent but Not Important, and Neither Urgent nor Important. This simple yet effective framework helps distinguish between tasks that require immediate attention and those that contribute to long-term goals.

Let's take a closer look at how you can use this matrix to effectively manage your tasks:

For reference, use this graphic:

	HIGH URGENT	SIGNIFICANT
HIGH	**DO** These are vital tasks with substantial urgency.	**SCHEDULE** These are critical tasks with minimal urgency.
IMPORTANCE	**NOT URGENT** **DELEGATE** These are pressing tasks with negligible impact.	**INSIGNIFICANT** **DELETE** These are trivial tasks with minor urgency.
LOW		

HIGH ━━━━━━━━━━━━━━ URGENCY ━━━━━━━━━━━━━━➤ LOW

Idea 1: Focus on tasks that align with your goals

The Eisenhower Matrix provides clarity by encouraging us to evaluate each task through the lens of urgency and importance. Imagine you have a list of tasks ranging from preparing a critical business proposal to responding to routine emails. By placing these tasks in their respective quadrants, you can see which ones truly align with your overarching goals, ensuring that your valuable time and resources are invested wisely.

Idea 2: Make Informed Decisions Using the Eisenhower Matrix

When faced with an onslaught of tasks, deciding where to focus can be daunting. The Eisenhower Matrix helps simplify this process, allowing you to make informed decisions about what needs immediate attention and what can wait.

Here is what you can do to get the most out of the Eisenhower Matrix for effective task prioritization:

- Start by listing all the tasks you need to accomplish.

- Assign a level of urgency and importance to each task. Urgency refers to tasks that require immediate attention, while importance refers to your long-term goals.

Place these tasks in the four quadrants of the Eisenhower Matrix:

- Urgent and Important (Quadrant I): Tasks that require immediate attention and high impact.

- Important but Not Urgent (Quadrant II): Tasks that contribute to long-term success but do not require immediate action.

- Urgent but Not Important (Quadrant III): Tasks that require immediate attention but have less impact on your goals.

- Neither urgent nor important (Quadrant IV): Low-impact tasks that often serve as distractions. By following these steps, you'll find yourself making more deliberate choices about where to focus your efforts, reducing the temptation to prioritize less important tasks (Eisenhower Matrix, n.d.).

Idea 3: Encourage Efficient Time Management

Implementing the Eisenhower Matrix helps individuals manage their time more efficiently by highlighting tasks that significantly increase productivity. Instead of getting bogged down in urgent but low-impact activities, you can focus on what's really important.

To use the matrix effectively:

Tackle Quadrant I tasks first because they are both urgent and high-impact.

- Dedicate regular time to Quadrant II tasks. These are critical for long-term success and growth. Activities such as strategic planning, capability development, and relationship building fall into this category.

- Delegate or minimize time spent on Quadrant III tasks. While these may seem urgent, they often divert attention from more meaningful work.

- Reduce or eliminate Quadrant IV activities. These tasks tend to waste time and provide little to no return on your investment.

This method ensures that you're spending your time on the tasks that matter most, thereby increasing your overall productivity.

Idea 4: Take a Strategic Approach to Productivity

The Eisenhower Matrix promotes a strategic approach to productivity by encouraging thoughtful resource allocation. By prioritizing tasks based on their importance, you can ensure that your efforts yield the highest returns.

Here's how to use the Eisenhower Matrix strategically:

- Review and update your to-do list regularly to ensure that you're focusing on the most important tasks.

- Be honest about the true urgency and importance of each task. Avoid inflating the importance of less critical tasks to justify procrastination.

- Set aside specific times to review and adjust your priorities. This will keep you focused on your goals and responsive to changing circumstances.

- Break down complex tasks into smaller, more manageable subtasks. This makes them easier to fit into the matrix and tackle.

By adopting these strategies, you'll be better equipped to handle multiple responsibilities without feeling overwhelmed. This structured approach not only increases productivity, but also promotes a sense of accomplishment and control.

The Eisenhower Matrix is an invaluable tool for anyone who wants to take control of their business and lifestyle. It provides a clear framework for distinguishing between urgent and important tasks, allowing you to make more informed decisions.

By implementing this matrix, you can effectively manage your time, reduce overwhelm, and achieve greater productivity aligned with your long-term goals.

Review your tasks regularly to ensure alignment with your strategic goals and adjust as needed. Effective task management involves prioritizing important tasks that drive progress, ensuring that time and resources are devoted to significant results. Recognizing that not all "urgent" tasks are important helps create a balanced approach to managing workload and preventing burnout.

To manage your tasks effectively:

- Regularly review and update your task lists to ensure alignment with your long-term goals.

- Delegate urgent but less important tasks to free up time for higher-value activities.

- Set clear boundaries to protect time for important tasks and minimize interruptions.

- Practice saying "no" to requests that don't align with your priorities to maintain a focused approach.

Mismanaging urgency and importance can lead to spending excessive time on low-value activities. To mitigate this, it's important to develop a keen sense of how to prioritize tasks. Focusing on high-impact actions will foster both professional growth and personal fulfillment.

Remember, being at the mercy of the latest and loudest is not a productive way to live. You're constantly putting out fires but never building anything of lasting value. You risk burning out and missing opportunities for deeper satisfaction and achievement.

The world may seem demanding, but when you take control of how you allocate your time and energy, you gain a sense of empowerment that's both liberating and fulfilling.

The Power of
Time-Blocking

Time-blocking is an incredible tool that can help you prioritize tasks and commitments more effectively, minimize overwhelm, and increase productivity. Despite our different roles, we all face the challenge of managing our time effectively.

Time-blocking is the practice of designating specific periods of time for specific tasks or activities, increasing efficiency by minimizing distractions and multitasking. This method serves as a protective barrier against the chaos of daily life, allowing for focused periods of work.

Think of it as building walls around your most important tasks to protect them from interruptions.

Refer to this image of time blocking when necessary:

08:00 Daily Planing / Management / Correspondence / Urgency	08:00 Daily Planing / Management / Correspondence / Urgency	08:00 Daily Planing / Management / Correspondence / Urgency	08:00 Daily Planing / Management / Correspondence / Urgency	08:00 Daily Planing / Management / Correspondence / Urgency
09:00 Meetings	09:00 Meetings	09:00 Meetings	09:00 Meetings	09:00 Meetings
09:30 Task	09:30 Task	09:30 Task	09:30 Task	09:30 Task
10:30 Break	10:30 Break	10:30 Break	10:30 Break	10:30 Break
11:00 Task	11:00 Task	11:00 Task	11:00 Task	11:00 Task
12:30 Lunch	12:30 Lunch	12:30 Lunch	12:30 Lunch	12:30 Lunch
13:30 Task	13:30 Task	13:30 Task	13:30 Task	13:30 Task
15:30 Break	15:30 Break	15:30 Break	15:30 Break	15:30 Break
16:00 Meetings	16:00 Meetings	16:00 Meetings	16:00 Meetings	16:00 Meetings
16:30 Task	16:30 Task	16:30 Task	16:30 Task	16:30 Task

Here is how to get started:

- **Start by identifying your major categories of tasks.** These might include work responsibilities, personal projects, exercise, or downtime. It's important to recognize what takes up your time.

- Next, **assign specific blocks of time to each category and task on your calendar.** For example, if you have a critical project at work, set aside uninterrupted hours in your schedule to tackle it head-on.

- **Fully commit to each block of time.** Eliminate any potential distractions, such as phone notifications or unnecessary meetings, during these times.

By scheduling blocks of time for different tasks, readers can prioritize activities based on importance and focus on one task at a time. This deliberate allocation of time ensures that high-priority items get the attention they deserve, while still allowing for balanced coverage of other areas.

Here's an effective way to do this:

- **Evaluate your to-do list** and rank tasks by urgency and importance.

- **Assign time slots** to the highest priority tasks first. That way, even if things go wrong later in the day, your most important tasks are already addressed.

- **Assign shorter, less intense block**s of time to lower priority tasks. This helps prevent burnout and keeps your energy level consistent throughout the day.

Implementing time blocks encourages better time management and reduces the likelihood of getting derailed by sudden distractions or shifting priorities. Imagine having a clear path for your day, reducing decision fatigue, and making it easier to say "no" to interruptions.

To make this practical:

- Start your day by reviewing your cluttered schedule. Adjust as needed, but try not to deviate too much.

- When unexpected tasks arise, assess their urgency. If possible, fit them into existing open blocks rather than rearranging your entire day.

- Be aware of your energy levels. Schedule demanding tasks when you're naturally more alert, and reserve easier tasks for when your energy drops.

Structuring the day with blocks of time increases productivity by creating a clear schedule that optimizes focus and minimizes interruptions. A well-structured day provides mental clarity and a sense of accomplishment, which promotes motivation and consistency.

Follow these three steps to structure your blocks of time:

1. **Dedicate the first hour of your day to planning and review.** This sets a purposeful tone and aligns your actions with your goals.

2. **Group similar tasks together.** This minimizes transition time and keeps you in the right mindset for certain types of work.

3. **Review your time blocks regularly** and adjust them based on feedback and results. The initial structure may need to be adjusted to better fit your workflow and preferences.

Done right, time blocks can be a game changer for two reasons:

1. **It allocates dedicated time to focus on tasks:** Ensure that each block is respected as sacred time for its intended task.

2. **It reduces multitasking by focusing on one activity at a time.** This increases productivity and leads to higher quality work.

One study found that moving to-do lists to calendars gave participants a greater sense of control over their workday (Harvard Business Review, 2018). Knowing exactly what you need to do and when helps combat the anxiety of an ever-growing to-do list and keeps you firmly in the driver's seat.

Notable individuals such as Elon Musk and Bill Gates have used time blocking to increase productivity (Holt, 2024). By breaking the day into intentional segments, they maximize focus and minimize multitasking.

Remember, time blocking isn't about rigidity, it's about mindful allocation. Embracing flexibility within a structured framework allows you to smoothly navigate unexpected changes while maintaining overall productivity.

Here's what you can do to get there:

First, choose a planner or digital tool. Options range from traditional paper planners to apps like Google Calendar or Trello.

Second, create a comprehensive list of your tasks and responsibilities. Include everything from work projects to personal commitments.

Third, prioritize these tasks. Determine which ones require immediate attention and allocate time accordingly.

Fourth, estimate the time it will take to complete each task and block it out in your planner. Be realistic so that you do not underestimate how long a task will take.

Fifth, make sure you include breaks. Consistent short breaks can refresh your mind and prevent burnout.

By incorporating these techniques, time management transforms from an abstract concept into a concrete, actionable strategy. Your days will become more focused, efficient, and less susceptible to the vagaries of distraction.

Integrating time blocking into your daily routine allows you to be more strategic with your time, resulting in increased productivity and reduced stress. It aligns your actions with your priorities and promotes a balanced approach that respects both professional and personal needs.

With practice and customization, this technique can significantly improve the way you manage your commitments and ultimately help you achieve your goals more effectively.

Pulling it Together for Effective Prioritization

As we have explored in this chapter, effectively prioritizing tasks and commitments is critical to managing our time and energy wisely.

Using techniques such as the Eisenhower Matrix, breaking large projects into manageable steps, and practicing time blocking can significantly reduce feelings of overwhelm. These methods allow us to focus on what really matters and ensure that our actions are aligned with long-term goals rather than simply reacting to immediate demands.

On a broader scale, mastering task prioritization not only increases personal productivity, but also contributes positively to workplace efficiency and academic success. It fosters a balanced lifestyle in which professional achievement and personal well-being coexist harmoniously.

Consider how adopting these strategies can transform your daily routine. By intentionally directing your focus and energy to high-value tasks, you pave the way for greater achievement and a more fulfilling life.

This journey toward effective task management is ongoing, evolving as you refine your approach and adapt to new challenges. Embrace this process with an open mind and let it lead you to sustainable growth and success.

Remember that your #1 goal is to use these tools and techniques to break away from the Shiny Object Syndrome that leads to distraction, noise and chaos.

Now, I'm going to teach you the ultimate hack for getting there...the POWER framework.

Implementing the POWER Framework

Many people today are caught in this cycle of busy activity, struggling to maintain focus amid countless competing demands on their time and energy. The challenge isn't just managing time, it's managing attention and sustaining it over time.

Enter the **POWER** framework, which provides *a systematic approach to cutting through the noise and increasing productivity.*

The problem many people face is not simply that they have too much to do, but rather that, they lack an effective strategy for managing those tasks efficiently.

Consider Sarah, a small business owner who spends her days juggling client meetings, marketing efforts, and administrative tasks. Despite her best efforts, she often feels like she's falling behind, unable to focus on high-priority tasks because she's constantly putting out fires.

Or how about John, an entrepreneur whose day is filled with interruptions - social media alerts, impromptu meetings, and the temptation to multitask just to stay ahead of the curve. Both Sarah and John represent countless others who need a structured way to regain control of their workdays and reduce stress while increasing productivity.

In this chapter, we will explore the detailed application of my POWER framework, which stands for **Prioritize, Organize**, **Weed** out distractions, **Establish** routines, **Reflect** and adjust.

We'll begin by discussing how to effectively prioritize tasks to ensure that your energy is focused on what's most important. Next, we'll look at how to systematically organize those tasks to make them more manageable and less daunting. We will then discuss how to eliminate distractions that interfere with your focus, followed by the importance of establishing consistent routines to support sustained productivity.

Finally, the chapter discusses the need for regular reflection and adjustment to keep you on track with your goals. By implementing this framework, you'll be better equipped to navigate a busy world with clarity and purpose.

Steps for Implementing the POWER Framework

Let's dive into the steps of the POWER framework for sustained focus. This method is designed to help you cut through the noise and streamline your efforts to get more done with less stress.

Prioritize tasks based on urgency and importance

First, let's talk about prioritizing tasks. Not all tasks are created equal. Understanding what needs immediate attention versus what can wait is critical. Think of it like triage in an emergency room: what's critical, what's important, and what's neither? You want to address what is both urgent and important first, and then move down the list.

Here is what you can do to accomplish this goal:

- Identify all the tasks you need to accomplish.

- Use a matrix system, such as the Eisenhower Box, to categorize these tasks into four quadrants: urgent and important, not urgent but important, urgent but not important, and neither urgent nor important.

- Focus your initial efforts on tasks that fall into the Urgent and Important category.

- Defer or delegate tasks in the other categories as needed.

By following this simple guideline, you will align your actions with your goals and reduce time wasted on less impactful activities.

Organize tasks systematically

Once you've prioritized your tasks, the next step is to organize them. An efficiently organized task list can make a huge difference. Imagine trying to find a document on a cluttered desk versus one that is neatly filed-the latter will save you time and mental energy.

Here are a few things you can do to systematically organize your tasks:

- Develop a consistent method for tracking tasks, whether it's a digital app or a physical planner.

- Break down large tasks into smaller, actionable steps. This makes daunting projects seem more manageable.

- Group similar tasks. This can be done by context (e.g. phone calls, emails) or by project.

- Set deadlines for each task or subset of tasks. This gives you a clear timeline and keeps you accountable.

A well-organized approach not only increases efficiency, but also provides clarity, making it easier to see progress and stay motivated.

Eliminate Distractions

Identifying and eliminating distractions is critical to maintaining focus. Distractions come in many forms-social media, unplanned meetings, or even too much multitasking. The goal is to create a work environment that is conducive to deep focus.

Here are some things you can do to eliminate distractions:

- Conduct an audit of your daily activities to identify common distractions.

- Use tools such as browser blockers or productivity applications to limit access to distracting websites and applications during work hours.

- Set specific times to check email or take breaks, rather than doing it on the fly throughout the day.

- Create a dedicated workspace free of non-work related items to signal to yourself and others that you are in "focus mode.

Eliminating distractions isn't about being rigid; it's about creating boundaries that protect your most valuable asset - your attention.

Establish Routines for Consistency and Productivity

Finally, establishing routines can greatly improve your consistency and productivity. A routine creates a rhythm that your mind and body get used to, which reduces decision fatigue and increases efficiency over time.

Here are some things you can do to create effective routines:

- Start your day with a morning routine that sets the tone for productivity. This could include activities such as exercise, planning your day, or a focused reading session.

- Set aside specific times for different types of work, such as creative tasks in the morning when you're fresh and administrative tasks in the afternoon.

- Incorporate rituals that signal the beginning and end of your workday. This can help your brain switch effectively between work and rest.

- Keep your sleep schedule consistent so you're well-rested and ready to tackle each day with energy.

A routine isn't a rigid schedule; it's a flexible framework that helps guide your daily actions toward your larger goals.

By integrating these components of the POWER framework-prioritizing, organizing, managing distractions, and establishing routines-you can build a sustainable model for maintaining focus.

Let's face it, it takes a little trial and error to find what works best, and that's okay. Regularly reflect on your methods, assess what can be improved, and adjust accordingly. Remember, the goal isn't perfection, it's progress.

Every step you take toward better focus is a step toward greater productivity and personal fulfillment. So go ahead, implement these strategies, and watch your focus increase and your stress decrease.

The Importance of Consistency in Using the POWER Framework

When we think about the POWER Framework, it's important to remember that its benefits are truly unlocked through consistent and repetitive application. I've found that consistency is not just about achieving a short-term burst of productivity; it's about setting the stage for long-term improvements in focus and decision-making.

Let's start with the first component: prioritization. It sounds simple enough-decide what's important and do it first. But the magic happens when this process is applied consistently.

The ability to prioritize effectively shapes our day-to-day decisions, creating a ripple effect in everything we do. Over time, this practice becomes ingrained in the way we approach tasks, turning prioritization from an occasional effort into an automatic response.

Here's what you can do to ensure consistent prioritization:

- Begin each day by identifying your most important tasks. Ask yourself what will have the greatest impact on your goals.

- Use tools such as Eisenhower matrices or task lists to visualize priorities and keep them top of mind.

- Always assess your progress at the end of the day by reflecting on what you have accomplished and reevaluating what remains to be done.

- Next, organize your tasks. Organization may seem simple, but it takes discipline to maintain it. Consistent organization helps reduce mental clutter, making it easier to find what you need when you need it. It also reduces cognitive load by creating systems that manage information efficiently without constant monitoring.

Develop consistent organizational habits:

- Create dedicated spaces for different types of tasks and materials, both digital and physical.

- Develop a filing system for documents and e-mail to streamline retrieval.

- Regularly review and update your organizational systems to ensure they remain effective as your needs evolve.

Now we move on to the practice of eliminating distractions. In a world full of potential interruptions, staying focused can feel like swimming upstream. With persistent effort, however, you can improve your ability to focus on the task at hand. Every time you successfully eliminate a distraction, you strengthen your ability to stay focused, creating a feedback loop that gets stronger over time.

To consistently eliminate distractions:

- Identify your top distractions and develop strategies to mitigate them. This could include setting specific times to check email or using applications that block distracting websites during work hours.

- Cultivate an environment conducive to focus, perhaps by using noise-canceling headphones or designating a quiet workspace.

- Establishing routines is another cornerstone of the POWER framework. Routines support sustained focus by incorporating productive behaviors into your daily life. When these routines become habitual, they create a stable foundation that reduces the mental energy required for decision-making, allowing you to reserve that brainpower for more complex tasks.

How to create and maintain effective routines:

- Start small by incorporating one new habit at a time, such as setting aside 10 minutes each morning for planning.

- Use cues to trigger routines. For example, drinking a cup of coffee can signal the start of your workday.

- Periodically review and adjust your routines to make sure they're still supporting your goals.

Reflection and adaptation complete the POWER framework. Consistent reflection allows you to identify what's working and make necessary adjustments. This iterative process ensures continuous improvement and keeps you focused on your larger goals.

When it comes to reflection and adaptation:

- Set regular intervals for evaluating your performance, whether weekly or monthly. Use these meetings to review your successes and challenges.

- Be flexible; allow your strategies to evolve based on what you learn.

- Seek feedback from others. They may offer perspectives you hadn't considered and help you refine your approaches.

The key lesson here is the transformative power of consistency within the POWER framework. By consistently applying prioritizing, organizing tasks, reducing distractions, establishing routines, and reflecting and adjusting, you build a robust structure for improved focus and productivity.

Remember, these methods aren't just one-time fixes, but practices that, when used regularly, will yield significant and lasting improvements in your efficiency and overall well-being. Stay committed to this framework, and over time you'll likely find that what initially required conscious effort has become second nature-a testament to the enduring power of consistency.

Tailoring the POWER Framework to Your Needs:

Adapting prioritization methods to fit personal goals and values is the first step in using the POWER framework. Prioritization becomes meaningful when it reflects what is truly important to you. That's why it's important to introspect and identify your core values and long-term goals.

For example, if you value family and health, make sure your daily tasks and projects reflect these priorities. Aligning work tasks with personal goals not only ensures consistency, but also keeps you motivated.

Consider using a values-based prioritization matrix that rates tasks based on how closely they align with your personal values and long-term goals.

Here is what you can do to achieve this alignment:

- Start by identifying your core values and big life goals.

- Break down these larger goals into smaller, more manageable tasks.

- Evaluate your current tasks or projects against these values and goals.

- Reorganize your to-do list to prioritize tasks that most closely align with your identified values.

- Periodically review and adjust your priorities to ensure continued alignment with evolving goals.

Tailoring organizational strategies to your unique work style and preferences can significantly increase productivity. A one-size-fits-all approach rarely works because everyone has different workflows and peak productivity times. Some people thrive on detailed to-do lists, while others find mind maps more intuitive. The key is to find what works best for you.

Here's how to develop an effective organizational strategy:

- Assess whether you are a visual thinker or prefer linear organization.

- Experiment with different tools, such as digital applications, bullet journals, or Kanban boards.

- Create a workspace that minimizes clutter but provides easy access to frequently used resources.

- Use color-coding or tagging systems to quickly find important information.

- Review and refine your organizational system regularly to adapt to changing needs.

Tailoring distraction management techniques to specific triggers and tendencies is another critical component. Distractions are inevitable, but recognizing and mitigating them can be transformative.

Here are some actionable steps to effectively manage distractions:

- Identify your primary sources of distraction by keeping a log of interruptions.

- Establish technology breaks by setting aside short windows to check messages after uninterrupted periods of work.

- Create physical barriers to highlight periods of focus, such as "do not disturb" signs or noise-canceling headphones.

- Use digital tools to limit access to distracting websites or applications during work hours.

Personalizing routines to maximize productivity and focus based on individual rhythms can make a significant difference in achieving sustained focus. Our natural energy levels fluctuate throughout the day, often following a biological rhythm known as the circadian cycle. Recognizing your high-energy periods and scheduling challenging tasks during those times can lead to better results.

Personalize your routine for maximum efficiency by:

- Tracking your energy levels over the course of a week to identify patterns of alertness and fatigue.

- Scheduling high-priority tasks during your peak productivity hours and reserving lower-effort activities for energy lulls.

- Taking regular breaks to prevent burnout and maintain high performance throughout the day.

- Using flexible work schedules when possible to align work demands with your natural rhythms.

- Making room for self-care practices such as exercise, adequate sleep, and hydration to support overall well-being.

Reflect and adjust your actions regularly to maintain focus and improve productivity. It's important to create a feedback loop where you consistently evaluate what's working and what's not.

Just as Cheryl Travers, PhD, found reflective goal setting to be effective in improving performance (APA, 2017), incorporating regular reviews of your processes and outcomes promotes continuous improvement.

To effectively implement reflective practices:

- Schedule weekly or bi-weekly review sessions to assess progress toward goals.

- Analyze what's contributing to success and identify areas that need change.

- Adjust your strategies based on these reflections and test new approaches as needed.

- Seek feedback from peers or mentors to gain outside perspectives and insights.

- Keep a reflective journal to track changes and continually learn from your experiences.

Tailoring the POWER framework to individual needs increases its effectiveness and relevance in promoting sustained focus.

By aligning prioritization with personal values, customizing organizational strategies, managing distractions according to specific triggers, and personalizing routines based on individual rhythms, you create a powerful strategy for maintaining high levels of productivity.

Reflecting on and adjusting these practices ensures continued alignment with goals, ultimately leading to more meaningful and sustainable results.

Reflection for Continuous Focus Improvement

When it comes to improving focus and productivity, reflection isn't just a nice-to-have-it's a cornerstone of success. The POWER framework-prioritize, organize, eliminate distractions, establish routines, reflect, and adjust-is designed for continuous improvement.

Let's explore how reflection can refine each aspect of this framework for sustained focus.

Reflect on past prioritization decisions to learn from successes and failures.

Reflection allows us to step back and evaluate our past choices. Did we prioritize effectively? What led to our successes and where did things go wrong?

For example, if you set out to complete a project but were distracted by other, less important tasks, reflection can help you determine what needs to be adjusted. Maybe there were urgent emails or meetings that seemed important at the time, but weren't aligned with your main goal. By analyzing these moments, you can identify patterns and prepare better strategies for future prioritization.

One study highlights the importance of reflection in learning from experience. Researchers found that coupling direct experience with intentional reflection significantly improved learning outcomes (Gino et al., 2014).

By reflecting on our prioritization process, we synthesize what worked and what didn't, ensuring that we make more informed decisions moving forward.

Use reflection to refine organizational methods and streamline task management processes.

Effective organization is critical to maintaining focus, but it's not a one-size-fits-all solution. Reflection helps us refine our methods. Perhaps your current system is a mix of digital tools and paper schedules, but you are still missing deadlines. Reflection might reveal that certain tools aren't as efficient as they should be, or perhaps a unified system would reduce friction and increase productivity.

Think about how often you find yourself searching for documents or reprioritizing tasks at the last minute. Upon reflection, you may find that setting up a more centralized filing system or adopting a project management tool like Trello or Asana could save time and reduce stress. Regularly evaluating and refining these methods based on past performance will keep your organizational skills sharp and responsive.

Analyze distraction patterns through reflection to identify recurring triggers and develop targeted strategies.

Distractions are inevitable, but understanding their origins can arm us with strategies to minimize them. Consider the common sources of your distractions: Is it social media notifications, impromptu conversations, or perhaps internal thoughts that pull you away from your tasks?

By identifying these triggers, you can create boundaries or rituals to protect yourself from them.

For example, if you find that you often lose focus when you check email first thing in the morning, consider setting aside specific times to manage email outside of your most productive hours.

Research supports that creating these reflective practices increases engagement and deepens participation in tasks (Mann, 2016). By recognizing patterns of distraction, you can create a workspace conducive to sustained focus.

Regularly evaluate and adjust routines based on reflection to optimize focus and productivity.

Routines provide structure, but they must be dynamic to remain effective. What works today may not be as effective tomorrow, so regular reflection is critical.

Evaluate your daily and weekly routines: Are there times of the day when you feel particularly unproductive? When do your energy levels peak, and how can you schedule challenging tasks around those times?

Continuous improvement requires us to be adaptable. Reflection reveals whether your current routines help or hinder your productivity. You may find that your pre-lunch routine leaves you sluggish-perhaps a short walk or an adjustment in your meal choices could revitalize that segment of your day. Reflective adjustments like these ensure that your routines evolve with your needs, improving overall productivity.

Key Takeaways

Reflection is not a passive activity; it's an active engagement with your experiences and practices. To truly benefit from the POWER framework, integrating reflection allows you to continually refine and adjust your approach to maintain sustained focus and growth.

By reflecting on past prioritization decisions, refining organizational methods, analyzing patterns of distraction, and regularly evaluating routines, you create a cycle of continuous improvement-a strategy firmly rooted in empirical evidence.

Backed by extensive research, using reflection to improve productivity is not just about looking back, but using that knowledge to drive future action. It's about turning experience into actionable insights that enable you to stay focused and consistently achieve your goals. This iterative process ensures that your methods remain relevant and effective, making reflection an essential component in the pursuit of productivity.

Final Thoughts on Implementing the POWER Framework

As we conclude our journey through the POWER framework, we've explored the critical steps needed to improve focus and productivity. Prioritizing based on urgency and importance lays the foundation and ensures that your efforts are focused on what really matters.

Systematic organization follows, providing a clear structure that supports efficiency. Eliminating distractions helps create an environment ripe for deep focus, free from the constant pull of interruptions. Establishing routines solidifies these practices and builds consistency into your daily life.

At this point, the evidence is clear: by consistently implementing and adapting these methods, you can achieve higher levels of focus and productivity. One concern, however, is that adopting new practices can seem overwhelming or daunting. It's important to start small, integrating one element at a time until it becomes a natural part of your routine.

Finally, remember that the POWER framework is more than a set of rules - it is a flexible system designed to evolve with your needs. Regular reflection and adaptation are key components that ensure continuous improvement and alignment with your goals.

As you move forward, embrace this framework with an open mind and you'll likely find that your focus sharpens, your productivity soars, and your stress diminishes. Keep experimenting, keep reflecting, and watch as small changes lead to significant, lasting impact.

PART 4:

Cultivating a Focused Work Environment and Turning Chaos into Clarity

"A bend in the road is not the end of the road... unless you fail to make the turn."

—*Helen Keller*

Introduction: From Chaos to Clarity

This section will provide practical advice and an actionable plan for transforming both your physical and digital workspaces into havens of productivity.

You'll learn how to declutter and organize your physical space by removing non-essential items and setting up designated zones for various tasks. You'll discover strategies for managing digital files and using tools to minimize online distractions, ensuring that your workspace supports your goals rather than hindering them.

By following this blueprint, you can create an environment that fosters deeper focus, reduces stress, and enhances your ability to achieve your objectives effectively, while reducing the risk of falling for Shiny Object Syndrome.

Creating Your Distraction-Free Environment

Visual clutter and digital interruptions are all too common in today's workspaces-both at home and on the road. Imagine walking into a room with stacks of paper everywhere, random objects scattered about, and a computer desktop filled with countless icons. Such an environment can lead to increased stress and decreased cognitive performance.

Imagine a workspace where everything has its place, unnecessary items are out of sight, and your digital files are neatly organized. Your mind isn't constantly bombarded with visual noise, which helps you focus and work more efficiently. In addition, constant notifications from social media and other online distractions can derail your concentration, leaving you frustrated and less productive.

This chapter offers practical advice for turning both your physical and digital workspaces into havens of productivity. You'll learn how to declutter and organize your physical space by removing unneeded items and creating designated zones for different tasks. You'll also discover strategies for managing digital files and using tools to minimize online distractions, so your workspace supports your goals, not hinders them.

By following these steps, you can create an environment that fosters deeper focus, reduces stress, and enhances your ability to effectively achieve your goals.

Declutter and Organize Your Workspace

As busy professionals, entrepreneurs, students, and individuals striving to increase productivity and focus, it's important to recognize how a well-organized workspace can significantly impact our efficiency and mental clarity.

First things first: removing unnecessary items and creating designated spaces for different tasks can help reduce visual distractions and improve mental clarity. Imagine walking into a cluttered room versus an organized one. The difference is immediately apparent. A clutter-free environment clears your mind and allows you to better focus on the task at hand.

Here's how to make it happen:

- Start by identifying the items on your desk or in your workspace that are essential for daily use. These are the things you reach for most often.

- Set aside a specific area for these essential items. This could be a special section of your desk or a special shelf.

- For items you use infrequently, find storage solutions such as bins or drawers to keep them out of sight but accessible when needed.

- Consider the layout of your workspace and designate zones for different activities. For example, designate one area for computer work, another for paperwork, and a third for brainstorming or creative thinking.

Next, let's talk about implementing a system for organizing documents and materials according to priority and frequency of use. This strategy can streamline your workflow and eliminate time-consuming searches.

Here's a guideline to get you started:

- Sort your documents into categories based on their importance and how often you need them. Create primary, secondary, and archive sections.

- For physical documents, use labeled folders or binders. Color-coding can also be very effective-assign specific colors to different types of documents (e.g., red for urgent, yellow for pending).

- For digital files, create a clear folder hierarchy on your computer or cloud storage. Start with broad categories, then break them down into more specific subfolders.

- Clean out these folders regularly, archiving outdated or less relevant files while keeping important documents current and easily accessible.

Regularly decluttering and organizing your workspace not only boosts productivity, but also promotes a sense of control and well-being. Think of it as resetting your environment. When everything is in its place, you naturally feel more in control, which makes it easier to tackle your tasks.

Using storage solutions such as shelves, bins, and digital folders can also help keep your workspace organized and focused. It's not just about having storage, it's about using it effectively. Here are some tips on how to use these tools to your advantage:

Invest in shelving that fits your space and allows you to store items vertically. This will maximize your available space and keep frequently used items within easy reach.

Bins can be a lifesaver for organizing small items that tend to clutter your desk, such as office supplies or charging cables. Clearly label each bin so you know exactly where to find what you need.

For digital organization, use apps and software designed for productivity. Tools like Trello, Evernote, or Google Drive can help you keep track of documents and tasks efficiently. Get in the habit of immediately saving new documents in their respective folders to keep things organized.

Streamlining your physical environment leads to mental clarity and increased efficiency at work. By taking deliberate steps to declutter, organize, and systematize your workspace-both physical and digital-you pave the way for a more focused, productive, and stress-free work experience.

Let's take a closer look at why there are such profound benefits to organizing our workspaces.

A cluttered space doesn't just mean a cluttered desk; it means a cluttered mind. When our physical environment is in disarray, it interferes with our ability to think clearly and prioritize effectively. Research supports this notion, showing that a cluttered workspace can contribute to higher stress levels and lower cognitive performance (Harvard Business Review, 2019).

On the flip side, maintaining a clean and organized workspace fosters a sense of accomplishment and positivity. Walking into a well-organized space can instantly lift your spirits and motivate you to get started on your tasks. You'll spend less time searching for misplaced items and more time focusing on what's important-your work.

But organization isn't a one-time event. It requires regular maintenance and a conscious effort to keep things in order.

Here are some tips for maintaining an organized workspace:

- Make it a habit to clean your desk at the end of each day. Put away papers, pens, and other items you used during the day.

- Set a reminder to clean more thoroughly once a week. Use this time to sort through accumulated clutter and reorganize as needed.

- Encourage a culture of cleanliness if you share your workspace with others. Promote the idea that everyone should take responsibility for keeping shared areas tidy.

- Schedule regular digital cleanups. Go through your computer files, e-mail, and digital documents to delete or archive what you don't need.

At its core, an organized workspace reflects an organized mind. It allows you to perform at your best, free from the distractions and stress that clutter brings. Whether you're a professional, entrepreneur, or student, these strategies can help you create an environment that supports your goals and increases your productivity.

Remember, the journey to a perfectly optimized workspace is an ongoing one. Start small, implement changes gradually, and stay committed to maintaining order. Before you know it, you'll be working more efficiently and feeling better equipped to handle whatever comes your way.

Effects of lighting, noise, and ergonomics

Optimizing both physical and digital workspaces can have a profound impact on productivity. The first factor to consider is lighting. Proper lighting that mimics natural daylight can reduce eye strain and fatigue, which in turn increases alertness and focus during work hours. It's not just about throwing more light into the room, it's about using the right kind of light.

Studies show that offices bathed in optimal light spectra improve concentration and minimize fatigue (Admin, 2024). Transitioning from harsh fluorescent lighting to softer, adjustable fixtures that mimic daylight can create an environment conducive to sustained productivity.

Simple steps like moving your desk closer to windows to take advantage of natural light or using adjustable LED lights can make a significant difference. Remember, it's not just about visibility; lighting affects circadian rhythms, which affect your cognitive function throughout the day.

Noise levels are another important element. Managing noise effectively can help create a peaceful work environment that is conducive to deep work and concentration.

For those who work in noisy environments, soundproofing materials or noise-canceling headphones can significantly reduce distractions. Research shows that high noise levels have a negative impact on productivity, especially for tasks that require deep concentration (Akbari et al., 2013).

Here's what you can do to manage noise levels:

- Use soundproofing materials, such as heavy curtains or wall panels, to absorb ambient noise.

- Noise-canceling headphones can be a game changer, especially for tasks that require deep concentration.

- If possible, designate a specific area for noisy activities and ensure that quiet zones remain undisturbed.

- Invest in white noise machines or apps if complete silence is not possible; surprisingly, consistent background noise can sometimes improve concentration better than intermittent interruptions.

Next, let's talk ergonomics. Ensuring that your furniture and equipment are ergonomically designed is paramount to maintaining physical comfort and reducing the risk of musculoskeletal problems. Ergonomic setups not only increase comfort, but also improve overall work efficiency.

Here's how to do this:

- Align your chair with your desk so your feet are flat on the floor and your knees are at a 90-degree angle.

- Position your computer screen at eye level, about an arm's length away to reduce neck strain.

- Be sure to use a chair that is designed for prolonged use and supports your lower back.

- Consider investing in ergonomic accessories such as keyboard trays, standing desks, or wrist supports to maintain a neutral posture.

Finally, don't underestimate the power of incorporating elements of nature into your workspace. Incorporating plants or soothing sounds can have a positive impact on mood and cognitive performance.

Plants have been shown to reduce stress levels and improve air quality, creating a fresher and more inviting workspace. A small green corner with low-maintenance plants such as succulents or peace lilies can bring a sense of calm and focus to your workspace.

Incorporating elements like these is not only aesthetically pleasing, it's empirically sound. Consider placing potted plants around your workspace or playing soft, nature-inspired background sounds to create a calming atmosphere.

Optimizing environmental factors such as lighting, noise, and ergonomics can significantly improve productivity and well-being in your workspace.

By paying attention to how lighting affects eye strain and energy levels, managing noise to promote better concentration, ensuring ergonomic alignment to support physical health, and integrating natural elements to improve mood and cognitive function, we can transform our workspaces into havens of productivity.

Digital tools that minimize distractions:

When it comes to optimizing workspaces, minimizing distractions is a major challenge. Let's explore some practical strategies, backed by empirical evidence, for creating an environment that promotes focus and productivity.

One effective way to control digital distractions is to use website blockers or applications that limit access to social media platforms. These tools are designed to help maintain focus by restricting access to distracting sites.

Applications such as StayFocusd and Reduce Distraction for Mac offer customizable settings that allow you to block specific websites or entire categories of sites during work hours (Temple University, 2024).

Here's what you can do:

- Install a reliable browser extension or app designed to reduce distractions.

- Adjust settings to block sites that waste your time.

- Within these apps, set schedules for when websites should be inaccessible to match your peak productivity times.

- Use features that turn off notifications to further minimize interruptions.

In addition to blocking websites, implementing time-tracking applications or techniques such as Pomodoro can significantly improve time management.

The Pomodoro technique involves working in focused intervals, typically 25 minutes, followed by short breaks. This method helps maintain high levels of concentration while providing regular rest periods to prevent burnout.

Apps like Focus Keeper on Android and iOS are excellent resources for this technique, allowing you to effectively schedule your "focus sessions" and breaks (Temple University, 2024).

To get started:

- Download a Pomodoro Timer app or use a simple kitchen timer.

- Plan your work in 25-minute intervals called Pomodoros.

- After each Pomodoro, take a 5-minute break to recharge.

- Take a longer break (15-30 minutes) after every four Pomodoros.

Setting digital alerts for essential tasks only and organizing email folders for efficient communication management can also reduce unnecessary interruptions. A cleaner inbox and fewer notifications means more uninterrupted time to focus on critical tasks.

According to research, setting up rules and filters in email clients can triage incoming emails, prioritizing urgent communications while deferring less important ones to a secondary folder (Maurer, 2019).

Here's how to streamline your digital notifications:

- Adjust the notification settings on your devices to only allow important notifications.

- Organize your email with folders for different types of communications.

- Create rules in your email client to automatically sort incoming messages into these folders.

- Designate specific times of the day to check and respond to email, rather than constantly monitoring your inbox.

Another important approach is to create designated digital workspaces or separate user accounts for work-related activities. By clearly delineating your personal and professional tasks, you create boundaries that help you focus on work during work hours and relax during personal time. This approach not only promotes a disciplined work routine, but also supports mental well-being by preventing work from spilling over into your personal life.

To implement this strategy, take the following steps:

- Set up separate user accounts on your computer for work and personal use.

- Customize each account with relevant applications, bookmarks, and desktop backgrounds to visually distinguish work and personal spaces.

- Log in to your work account during business hours and switch to your personal account during non-business hours.

- Ensure that work-related notifications and e-mail are routed only to your work account.

Using technology to reduce distractions can make your workday more productive and focused. Given the complexity and variety of distractions in a digital workspace, it is critical to take proactive steps to manage your environment.

From blocking unproductive websites and using the Pomodoro Technique to better managing your email and separating work and personal digital spaces, these strategies are backed by strong evidence and offer practical benefits.

By adopting these habits and tools, busy professionals, entrepreneurs, and students alike can cultivate an optimal digital workspace that supports both economic growth and human well-being.

Personal responsibility is key, but a safety net of productivity tools ensures a balanced approach to the demands of the modern digital landscape.

Strategies for setting boundaries

Setting work hours and communicating boundaries with colleagues or family members can help create a focused, uninterrupted work environment. Imagine trying to complete an important project and being constantly interrupted by children asking for snacks, a spouse bringing up household chores, or friends wanting to chat because they assume you're always available. To avoid these interruptions and create a more productive workspace, it is important to set clear boundaries.

Here are some things you can do to set them:

- Clearly communicate your work hours to your household members. Let them know when you won't be available and set rules around those times.

- Use a digital calendar to share your schedule with colleagues, friends, or family members to make sure everyone knows when you're in work mode.

- Reinforce these boundaries consistently. If someone interrupts you during work hours, gently remind them of the established rules. Over time, this will help solidify the expectation that your work hours are as sacrosanct as if you were in a traditional office.

Setting clear daily goals and time-blocking schedules can guide work priorities and provide specific time slots for deep, uninterrupted work sessions.

Think of your day as a series of blocks dedicated to specific tasks, much like a well-organized filing cabinet. When each block has a defined purpose, it's easier to maintain focus and avoid distractions.

Here is what you can do to achieve this goal:

- At the beginning of each day, identify your main goals. Identify one or two key tasks that are non-negotiable and must be accomplished.

- Designate specific time slots on your calendar for these tasks. This practice, often referred to as "time blocking," helps you focus your attention on high-priority activities without straying into less critical tasks.

- Setting aside time for other responsibilities, such as meetings, email, or administrative work, ensures that each task gets the attention it deserves without overwhelming any part of your day.

Creating physical barriers, such as closed doors or visual cues that signal focus time, can deter distractions and signal to others that you are in work mode. Even if you don't have a separate home office, there are ways to create visual and physical cues that indicate when you don't want to be disturbed.

Here are a few things you can do to start the process:

- Use closed doors, if you have them. The simple act of closing a door can create a psychological barrier that tells others that you are not to be disturbed.

- If a door is not an option, use visual cues such as a sign or a physical object such as a lamp that, when turned on, communicates your need for privacy.

- Locate your workspace away from common areas where interruptions are likely. Position your desk in a quiet corner or facing a wall to minimize visual distractions.

Maintaining a distraction-free workspace isn't just about blocking out the noise; it's about intentionally designing your environment and managing your time to foster deeper focus and greater achievement.

When you set boundaries and thoughtfully structure your day, you build a strong foundation that balances both personal freedom and social responsibility. This dual approach ensures that while you prioritize your tasks and productivity, you also respect the needs of those around you-whether family members or colleagues-and promote a balanced and healthy work-life integration.

Ultimately, the goal is to create a workspace-whether physical or digital-that aligns with your professional and personal goals. This alignment not only paves the way for greater productivity, but also fosters a healthier and more balanced work-life experience.

As you move forward, stay adaptable and attentive to your evolving needs to ensure your workspace continues to support you in doing your best work.

Constructing Your Deep Work Mindset

Imagine a world where you could accomplish your most important tasks without distractions pulling you in every direction.

In our current reality of constant notifications and interruptions, finding moments of deep focus seems nearly impossible. Many professionals, entrepreneurs, and students yearn to break free from this cycle and immerse themselves in deep, focused work.

The modern workplace is full of challenges that make uninterrupted focus difficult to achieve. Emails, meetings, social media, and countless other distractions constantly vie for our attention. These interruptions not only hinder productivity, but also lead to increased stress and burnout.

This chapter explores strategies for cultivating a deep work mindset that enables you to minimize distractions and focus intently on what really matters.

It explores practical techniques such as time blocking, establishing focused work routines, and setting clear priorities. You will also learn about the benefits of deep work, including improved cognitive performance, increased productivity, and greater job satisfaction.

By incorporating these methods into your daily life, you can transform your approach to work, achieve more meaningful results, and enjoy a sense of fulfillment and accomplishment.

Focused Work and the State of Flow

Focused work is the cornerstone of productivity and success. In an age of distractions, the ability to focus deeply on important tasks has never been more important.

When we focus intensely, we enter a state of heightened efficiency where our best work happens. It's not just about getting more done; it's about making meaningful progress toward our most important goals.

Research underscores the direct link between focused work and improved performance. Mihaly Csikszentmihalyi's concept of "flow" highlights how being fully immersed in a task enhances creativity and productivity (University of Southern California, 2016).

In this state of flow, we produce our highest quality work, making every minute count far more than in a scattered state of mind.

Deep Work and Doing the Hard Things First

Doing the hard things first is another critical component of maximizing productivity through focused work. When we prioritize difficult tasks at the beginning of our workday, we are using our peak cognitive capacity. These early hours are often when we're most alert and capable, making it easier to combat procrastination and avoid the pitfall of Shiny Object Syndrome (SOS).

The practice of deep work aligns seamlessly with this approach. By devoting undistracted time to complicated and mentally demanding activities, we not only ensure that they get done, but also improve their quality.

Cal Newport's book "Deep Work: Rules for Focused Success in a Distracted World" illustrates this point beautifully. Newport emphasizes that high-value tasks require sustained attention and minimal interruptions to truly excel (America et al., n.d.).

Consider, for example, Adam Grant, a Wharton professor known for his immense productivity. Grant's strategy is to divide his difficult tasks into focused, distraction-free periods.

As a result, he achieves exceptional results without necessarily working longer hours than his peers, proving that quality trumps quantity when it comes to productivity (America et al., n.d.).

Incorporating these strategies into your routine can transform your work life.

Here are some ways to get started:

- Create a daily schedule that includes time for uninterrupted deep work.

- Schedule your most challenging tasks for the times of day when you're most alert.

- Minimize distractions by turning off notifications, setting boundaries with colleagues, and creating a dedicated workspace.

By understanding and implementing these principles, you can significantly improve your productivity and make measurable progress toward your goals. The key is consistency and a conscious effort to cultivate an environment conducive to deep work. Over time, these habits will become second nature, leading to greater achievement and a more satisfying professional life.

Embracing the Deep Work Philosophy

Developing the ability to focus deeply on important work and minimize distractions is a critical skill in today's fast-paced world. Cal Newport's philosophy of deep work provides valuable insights into how we can achieve this. Newport defines deep work as the ability to focus on a cognitively demanding task without distraction, an increasingly rare but highly valuable skill.

One of the main benefits of deep work is improved cognitive performance. When you train your brain to focus intensely on a single task, you build neural pathways that enhance your ability to think deeply and critically. This kind of mental conditioning allows you to solve complex problems more effectively, innovate, and produce high-quality work.

Another important benefit is increased productivity. In an environment filled with constant notifications, emails, and social media pings, it's easy to get caught up in "shallow work"-tasks that are easy but not necessarily impactful.

By dedicating specific blocks of time to deep work, you can accomplish more meaningful tasks in less time. This focused approach helps eliminate the cycle of procrastination, making way for consistent progress toward your goals.

Greater job satisfaction is another notable benefit of deep work. When you're deeply engaged in your work, you're more likely to enter a state of flow-a psychological state in which you're fully immersed and enjoying the process. This intrinsic reward can make even challenging tasks feel more fulfilling, leading to greater overall job satisfaction and well-being.

To maximize the benefits of deep work, consider these practical steps:

- Identify your most important tasks: Determine which tasks require your full attention and block out time for them.

- Eliminate distractions: Create an environment conducive to focus by turning off notifications, using apps that limit Internet access, or finding a quiet workspace.

- Set clear goals: Define what you want to accomplish during your deep work sessions. Having clear goals will help you stay focused and measure your progress.

- Take regular breaks: Balance intense focus with breaks to refresh your mind. Techniques like the Pomodoro Technique can be helpful.

- Create rituals: Develop routines before you begin deep work to signal your brain that it's time to focus. This can be as simple as a few minutes of meditation or a quick review of your goals.

By implementing these strategies, you can cultivate the ability to engage in deep work and reap its many benefits. This approach not only increases your productivity, but also contributes to your overall sense of accomplishment and well-being in both your professional and personal life.

Set clear goals and priorities

Developing the ability to focus deeply on important work and minimize distractions requires a structured approach. Goal setting is critical to laying the foundation for this process.

Goal Setting

- Clear, actionable goals: To achieve intense focus, you need to set clear, actionable goals that are aligned with your long-term objectives. Here's what you can do:

- First, identify what you want to accomplish and make sure it aligns with your larger life or career goals.

- Second, break down those larger goals into smaller, more manageable tasks.

- Third, write each task down clearly to avoid ambiguity.

- Fourth, review your goals regularly and adjust them as needed to stay on track.

One of the most effective ways to set these goals is to use the SMART criteria: Specific, Measurable, Achievable, Relevant, and Time-Bound (Tips for Setting SMART Goals | University of Missouri System., n.d.). This framework ensures that each goal you set is specific and achievable, which is essential for maintaining focus and motivation.

- Specific: Be specific about your goal. Instead of saying, "I want to improve my skills," say, "I want to complete an online data analysis course within three months."

- Measurable: Establish criteria for tracking your progress. For example, determine how many modules you need to complete each week to complete the course on time.

- Achievable: Make sure your goal is realistic given your current resources and constraints. If the course requires ten hours of study per week and you only have five, you may need to adjust your schedule.

- Relevant: Balance your goal with other relevant goals. If you're looking to advance your career, choose courses that directly contribute to your desired role.

- Time-bound: Set a clear deadline. A goal without a timeframe lacks urgency. By specifying when you'll complete the course, you create a sense of commitment and purpose.

Build a Focused Work Routine with Time Blocking

Time blocking is a powerful strategy that allows us to structure our days for maximum focus by dedicating specific time slots to different tasks.

By grouping similar tasks into designated blocks, we minimize the cognitive load of constantly switching between different types of work. This method not only increases productivity, but also creates a sense of accomplishment as we check off completed blocks one at a time.

To create an effective time-blocked schedule, start by identifying your most important tasks and setting aside uninterrupted periods for deep work. Begin with a weekly overview and mark important meetings and deadlines.

From there, assign specific blocks of time to major projects to ensure you have ample stretches of uninterrupted time. Build in breaks to recharge and buffer time to handle unexpected tasks.

A consistent morning routine sets the tone for a productive day and provides a stable foundation from which to tackle daily challenges. A well-structured morning helps optimize mental clarity, boosts energy levels, and fosters a positive attitude that carries throughout the day.

Establishing a routine may feel mundane at first, but it significantly improves overall productivity and health (Establishing a routine can have huge benefits for your life. Here are 5 ways to do it. World Economic Forum, n.d.).

Key components of an effective morning routine include exercise, mindfulness practices, and planning. Exercise invigorates the body and mind, preparing you to face the day with vigor. Incorporating mindfulness techniques, such as meditation or deep breathing, helps reduce stress and increase focus.

Here's what you can do to build a strong morning routine:

- Start your day early to enjoy some quiet time before the usual rush begins.

- Get some physical activity, even if it's just a brisk walk or a quick workout, to boost energy levels.

- Spend a few minutes in mindfulness, practicing meditation or simple breathing exercises to clear your mind.

- Set aside time for creative activities, such as journaling or reading, to stimulate your brain.

- Plan your tasks for the day. Outline your priorities and set clear intentions for what you want to accomplish.

This combination of physical, mental, and strategic activities will ensure that you start your workday on a high note and are equipped to maintain focus and productivity throughout the day.

Implementing time blocking and a solid morning routine requires commitment and consistency, but the rewards in terms of productivity and mental clarity are significant.

These two strategies streamline your workflow, reduce distractions, and empower you to take charge of your day, ultimately leading to greater accomplishment and personal satisfaction.

Techniques to Improve Focus

Developing the ability to focus deeply on important work and minimize distractions is critical in today's fast-paced environment. This section provides strategies to help you cultivate this skill and increase your productivity.

Mindfulness and Meditation

Mindfulness practices: Simple exercises to improve focus and awareness can be a game changer. Being mindful means being present and fully engaged in whatever you're doing. It allows you to push aside distractions and give your full attention to the task at hand.

Here are some practical mindfulness exercises you can incorporate into your daily routine:

- Several times a day, take 60 seconds to focus only on your breathing. If your mind wanders, gently bring it back to your breath.

- Pick an object around you and give your full attention to observing it without analyzing or labeling it. Notice its color, shape, and texture.

- Slowly count to ten in your mind. If you become distracted, begin again until you reach ten without any interruption from your thoughts.

- Eat your meals slowly, savoring each bite. Pay close attention to the taste, smell, and texture of your food. Practicing this during meals can greatly increase your overall mindfulness throughout the day.

- Meditate: The benefits of meditation for improving focus and reducing mental clutter are supported by numerous studies. According to research published by Penn State World Campus, mindfulness not only increases focus, but also reduces stress (Voices, P., 2014). Even short periods of meditation can lead to significant improvements in attention and emotional regulation.

If you're new to meditation, getting started can feel a little overwhelming. But remember, everyone starts somewhere. Start with just a few minutes a day and gradually increase the duration as you become more comfortable.

Here is a three-step process for effective meditation:

- Find a quiet place where you won't be disturbed. Sit comfortably and close your eyes.

- Focus on your breathing. Notice the sensation of air entering and exiting your nostrils. If your mind wanders - and it will - gently bring your attention back to your breath.

- Use guided meditation apps or recordings if you find it difficult to meditate on your own. These resources can provide structure and guidance.

Research has shown that even short sessions of mindfulness meditation can improve attentional control and reduce stress levels in novices (Creem et al., 2018). So incorporating meditation into your daily routine can have a profound effect on your ability to focus deeply and stay productive.

The Pomodoro Technique

An overview of the Pomodoro Technique: This time management method is a simple yet effective way to maintain focus and combat procrastination. The core idea is to divide your work into chunks, traditionally 25 minutes in length, separated by short breaks. These intervals are called "pomodoros," named after the tomato-shaped kitchen timer used by the technique's inventor, Francesco Cirillo.

Application: Using the Pomodoro Technique can help you maintain sustained focus without burning out. Here's how to use it:

- Pick a task to work on.

- Set a timer for 25 minutes and focus only on that task until the timer goes off.

- Take a short break, about 5 minutes, to rest and clear your mind.

- After completing four Pomodoros, take a longer break of 15-30 minutes to recharge.

This technique helps create a sense of urgency, which makes it easier to commit to uninterrupted work during the pomodoro. It also provides regular breaks to prevent mental fatigue and keep your mind fresh.

Incorporating these strategies into your daily routine can significantly increase your ability to focus deeply and minimize distractions. By practicing mindfulness and meditation, you can improve your concentration and reduce stress. The Pomodoro Technique can help you manage your time effectively and stay productive. Together, these methods can empower you to be more focused at work and live a more balanced, fulfilling life.

Overcome common challenges

Managing interruptions

Interruptions are an inevitable part of our daily lives, whether they come from colleagues, emails, or personal phone calls. For busy professionals, entrepreneurs, and students, minimizing these interruptions is critical to maintaining focus and getting important work done.

Strategies for Minimizing Interruptions:

Effective management starts with setting boundaries and clearly communicating your availability.

Here are five steps that can help:

1. Create a dedicated workspace: Designate an area where you can work without distractions. This signals to others that you're focused and not to be disturbed.

2. Set clear boundaries: Communicate your work hours to family, friends, and colleagues. Let them know when you're available and when you're not.

3. Use signals: Simple signs like "Do Not Disturb" can be effective in letting people know when you're deep in the weeds.

4. Schedule interruptions: Set aside specific times to check email and messages. By scheduling these tasks, you can avoid constant interruptions.

5. Use technology: Use apps and tools that block notifications during focused periods. These can be invaluable in limiting digital distractions.

Deal with unavoidable interruptions

Despite your best efforts, some interruptions are unavoidable. The key is to manage them efficiently and quickly regain your focus.

1. Acknowledge and pause: When you're interrupted, acknowledge the person politely and let them know you'll get back to them. This helps reduce the immediate pressure.

2. Have a plan to resume: Before you address the interruption, write down where you left off and your next step. This technique provides cognitive closure, allowing you to return to your task more seamlessly (Glomb et al., 2020).

3. Re-focus quickly: After the interruption, take a moment to refocus. Deep breathing or a quick stretch can help reset your mind.

4. Limit discussions: If possible, keep the interruption short. Offer to resume the discussion at a later, scheduled time.

Managing Mental Fatigue

Mental fatigue is often a silent productivity killer. It is important to recognize its signs and know how to effectively recover.

Recognize the Signs of Mental Fatigue

Mental fatigue manifests itself in a variety of ways, including difficulty concentrating, frequent yawning, irritability, and a feeling of mental heaviness. It's important to recognize these signs early to prevent a significant drop in productivity.

Recovery Strategies

Restoring your mental energy can be simple, yet profoundly effective.

Here are four restorative strategies:

1. Short naps: A short nap of 10 to 30 minutes can rejuvenate your cognitive function without interfering with your nighttime sleep.

2. Exercise: Physical activity increases blood flow to the brain, which improves overall alertness and mood. Even a short walk can make a big difference.

3. Deep Breathing: Practicing deep breathing exercises helps relax the mind and body, reducing stress and promoting clarity.

4. Scheduled breaks: Build regular breaks into your routine to prevent burnout. These intervals allow you to rest and reset before diving back into work.

Balancing mental well-being with productivity requires conscious effort and techniques. By mastering the art of managing interruptions and recognizing mental fatigue, you can create an environment conducive to deep, focused work.

Maintaining a Focused Work Mindset

Continuous improvement and building resilience

Regular reflection is key for anyone who wants to improve their ability to focus deeply on important work. Taking time to reflect on which strategies worked well and which didn't can provide invaluable insight.

Here is a simple system you can implement to achieve continuous improvement:

1. First, set aside regular intervals-weekly or monthly-to evaluate your productivity habits.

2. Second, keep a journal in which you record daily successes and setbacks.

3. Third, look for patterns in your reflections. These patterns will help you identify what consistently helps your focus and what derails it.

4. Finally, don't be afraid to experiment with new approaches. Adjusting and tweaking your techniques based on these reflections can lead to more efficient ways of working.

Adjusting strategies is the next logical step after reflection. Life isn't static, and neither should your methods for maintaining deep focus. Circumstances change, and so should your approach.

When you notice that something isn't working as effectively as it once did, it's time to make a change. Listen to yourself-your energy levels, your focus spans-and be willing to pivot accordingly.

- Start by setting achievable short-term goals to test new methods.

- Collect data on how these new approaches affect your productivity.

- Compare this data to your previous methods to see if there has been an improvement.

- Be open to discarding what doesn't work and doubling down on what does.

Developing a growth mindset plays a critical role in maintaining long-term focus. Viewing challenges as opportunities rather than setbacks can change your perspective. When a task seems daunting, remember that it's a chance to grow.

Instead of shying away from difficulty, embrace it. Believing that skills can be developed through dedication and hard work fosters resilience, which is essential for sustained focus.

Managing stress is essential to maintaining productivity and focus over time. Stress can derail even the most focused individuals. Techniques for managing stress include mindfulness practices, exercise, and proper rest.

Here's how to manage stress effectively:

1. Get regular physical activity. Exercise helps reduce stress hormones and increases endorphins, which improve mood.

2. Practice mindfulness. Simple exercises like deep breathing or guided meditation can calm your mind and reduce anxiety.

3. Get enough sleep. A well-rested mind is better able to focus for longer periods of time.

4. Don't hesitate to seek professional help if you need it. Counseling or therapy can provide additional strategies tailored to your specific needs (Mayo Clinic Staff, 2020).

Continually honing your skills through regular reflection and adaptation, coupled with building resilience through a growth mindset and effective stress management, creates a robust framework for minimizing distractions and focusing deeply on important work.

Integrating Focused Work into Daily Life

Throughout this chapter, we have explored several strategies for developing the ability to focus deeply on important work and minimize distractions.

We discussed the importance of focused work, supported by Mihaly Csikszentmihalyi's concept of flow, which emphasizes the link between deep focus and increased creativity and productivity.

Tackling challenging tasks first and incorporating strategies such as time blocking and mindfulness exercises were highlighted as effective ways to maintain sustained attention.

Returning to our earlier discussion, deep work plays a critical role in achieving high productivity and satisfaction. By prioritizing essential tasks and minimizing interruptions, you can tap into your peak cognitive abilities and produce more meaningful results.

However, it's important to recognize that establishing and maintaining a focused work routine can be challenging. Factors such as physical and mental fatigue, external interruptions, and shifting priorities can disrupt even the most well-planned schedules. Understanding and anticipating these challenges allows you to develop resilience and adapt effectively.

On a broader scale, mastering the art of deep work can have a significant impact not only on individual productivity, but also on organizational success and overall well-being. By fostering an environment where deep work is valued and supported, teams can thrive and reach their highest potential.

While cultivating deep focus and reducing distractions requires conscious effort and continuous improvement, the rewards are profound. As you integrate these principles into your daily routine, consider how they align with your personal goals and professional responsibilities. The path to greater productivity is not just about working harder, it is about working smarter.

Embrace the process, remain adaptable, and continue to strive for a balance that fosters both individual growth and collective success.

The 'Power of Decision' Trees

When faced with complex decisions, the brain often struggles to process numerous variables at once. Deciding whether to accept a job offer, for example, involves weighing factors such as salary, work-life balance, growth opportunities, and company culture.

Without a clear framework, such decisions can feel paralyzing. Many people fall prey to "shiny object syndrome," jumping at attractive but potentially irrelevant options only to regret it later.

The lack of clear processes can lead to impulsive decisions that result in missed opportunities or unintended consequences. The gravity of these decisions underscores the need for systematic tools that demystify complexity and provide actionable insights.

This chapter examines practical methods for bringing clarity to decision making. By exploring tools such as decision trees and the role of intuition, you will learn to blend analytical reasoning with subconscious insights to present a holistic approach to decision making.

By mastering these techniques, you will equip yourself to navigate life's complex choices with confidence, precision, and foresight. Through this journey, you'll discover the balanced interplay between logic and intuition, empowering you to make well-rounded and informed decisions in both your personal and professional lives.

Use decision trees to effectively manage complex decisions

Decision trees help you visualize the potential outcomes and implications of your choices so you can make more informed decisions. For anyone struggling with distractions, the noise can make evaluating options feel like navigating a foggy forest.

Decision trees are like clearing that fog, providing a road map to follow.

Here's how to use them effectively:

- Identify the decision you're facing. It could be anything from where to invest your time to which project to prioritize at work.

- Break down the big decision into smaller, more manageable components. Think of them as branches growing from the trunk of a tree.

- Evaluate each branch by considering its possible outcomes. Use real-world data, where available, to ensure that your insights are based on reality, not assumptions.

- Weigh the pros and cons of each outcome. This visual representation helps you see all possible paths clearly and provides a holistic view.

Decision trees provide a structured approach to evaluating different options and their consequences. They lay out options in a way that is easy to digest, almost like turning complex word problems into simple arithmetic. Imagine having a plan that reduces uncertainty and allows you to anticipate hurdles before they become full-blown problems.

By using decision trees, you can improve your analytical skills and decision-making processes. With practice, you'll become more adept at analyzing issues logically, leading to more thoughtful strategies in both your personal and professional life.

The focus here is on cultivating a habit - over time, your mind will begin to construct these trees naturally, even without pen and paper.

Decision trees provide a systematic way to consider different factors and weigh the pros and cons of each choice. When every decision feels critical, overthinking can paralyze progress. These trees help untangle complex thoughts and give due consideration to each factor without feeling overwhelmed.

For example, suppose you're deciding whether to accept a new job offer. Your decision tree might start with the job offer at the top. Branches might break down into considerations such as salary, work-life balance, company culture, and career growth. Under each of these, additional branches could detail specifics such as commute times, remote work policies, team structure, and advancement opportunities.

The methodical layout ensures that nothing is overlooked and allows for a comprehensive assessment. As you move through each branch, balanced decisions become attainable, reducing stress and paving the way for clear, confident decisions.

Key Takeaways: Decision trees provide a methodical approach to decision-making that allows you to fully evaluate alternatives. By internalizing this tool, you'll arm yourself against impulsiveness and ensure that decisions are based on evidence and thorough analysis.

Understand the role of intuition in decision making

Intuition can serve as a valuable complement to analytical processes, providing insights that logic may miss. Take a moment to think about the last time you had a gut feeling about something - perhaps it was an opportunity at work or a decision in your personal life.

Often these intuitive moments come from our subconscious mind processing information and past experiences in ways we may not be immediately aware of. When we allow intuition to inform our analytical processes, we tap into a resource that can reveal nuances and possibilities that pure logic might miss.

It's important to understand that intuition is not just a hunch; it's a synthesis of knowledge, experience, and subtle cues picked up over time.

For example, when experienced investors make decisions, they don't just rely on financial data. They also rely on their intuitive sense of market trends, based on years of observation and practice. This blend of intuition and analysis allows them to make more dynamic and informed decisions.

Developing intuition through practice and mindfulness can lead to more confident decision-making.

Here are three steps you can take to sharpen your intuitive skills:

1. Regularly reflect on past decisions: Review past decisions in which you relied on your intuition. Analyze the results and the factors that led to those intuitive insights. This reflection sharpens your ability to recognize intuitive patterns.

2. Engage in activities that promote creativity and relaxation: Activities such as journaling, drawing, or even taking long walks can help unlock your intuitive mind. These practices encourage a free flow of ideas that can later be translated into intuitive insights.

3. Find quiet moments: Create pockets of silence in your daily routine. This can be as simple as taking five minutes to sit quietly without distraction. These moments of stillness allow you to tune into your inner signals.

Balancing intuition with rational analysis can lead to well-rounded and informed decisions. It's like having two powerful tools at your disposal. Logic provides structure and evidence-based reasoning, ensuring that decisions are grounded and objective. On the other hand, intuition adds depth and a holistic view, capturing the subtleties that raw data might miss.

Returning to our earlier analogy of navigating through a foggy forest, decision trees act as a much-needed clearing, revealing the path ahead.

By incorporating decision trees into your routine, you give yourself a powerful tool to analyze issues logically and make informed decisions. This practice not only fosters better strategies, but also instills a habit of organized thinking that can be applied to various aspects of life.

It's important to recognize, however, that while decision trees are a powerful tool for clarifying choices, readers may find the initial implementation challenging. The process takes diligence and practice to become second nature.

There will be moments of doubt, or instances where the sheer complexity of the decisions may seem overwhelming. But it's in these moments that decision trees prove their worth by untangling thoughts and clearly presenting options.

As we wrap up this chapter, consider the broader implications of integrating decision trees into your life. It's not just about making decisions-it's about fostering a mindset that thrives on clarity and structured thinking. Embrace this tool and let it guide you through the fog of complexity to clearer, calmer, and more confident decision-making.

The Power of Saying
No

Saying no is a critical skill in today's world of distractions and demands. The power of saying no allows you to maintain focus and direct your energies toward meaningful goals. Learning to say no can prevent the derailment of long-term goals by resisting the temptation of quick rewards or attractive but irrelevant tasks. This ensures that attention remains focused on what matters, leading to better results and personal satisfaction.

The ability to say no is essential to controlling shiny object syndrome (SOS). Saying no isn't just about saying no; it's a powerful tool for eliminating distractions and prioritizing meaningful tasks that align with your goals.

The Importance of Saying No

First, saying no helps eliminate distractions from new opportunities that do not align with your long-term goals. New and tempting opportunities often arise that promise quick rewards or interesting diversions. However, engaging in these distractions often derails progress toward your primary goals. By rejecting such offers, you can protect your plans from distraction.

A disciplined approach to rejecting unrelated activities ensures that your efforts are focused on what matters. Consistently reminding yourself of the bigger picture reduces the appeal of irrelevant pursuits.

This practice cultivates a mindset in which every potential commitment is scrutinized for its relevance to overarching goals.

Saying no thus serves as a protective barrier against the time-consuming lure of SOS.

For example, students juggling numerous club memberships and part-time jobs can benefit immensely from narrowing their commitments to fewer, more relevant activities. This not only improves academic performance, but also enriches personal development in chosen areas.

Progress toward long-term goals requires commitment and perseverance. By limiting involvement to goal-oriented activities, you are more likely to see continuous improvement and achieve milestones efficiently. This disciplined approach not only accelerates achievement, but also ensures that deviations are minimized.

Setting boundaries increases mental clarity and reduces the likelihood of being overwhelmed by multiple commitments. Clear boundaries create space for thoughtful decision making and effective problem solving. When the mind is cluttered with too many commitments, cognitive function suffers, which affects overall performance.

Psychological Barriers to Saying No

One of the primary psychological barriers to saying no is fear of missing out (FOMO). FOMO creates a pervasive sense of anxiety when individuals consider turning down opportunities. This fear stems from the concern that declining an invitation or offer will result in missing out on an important experience or falling behind others who choose to participate.

This can lead to over-commitment in professional settings as individuals feel compelled to accept every opportunity presented to them for fear of missing out on potential advancement, networking opportunities, or significant projects.

Constantly saying yes to avoid FOMO can quickly overwhelm your schedule, reducing productivity and focus.

The desire for approval is another significant barrier to saying no to requests. Humans have an innate need for social acceptance and validation from peers and superiors. This desire often drives individuals to take on tasks and commitments, even when they push their limits.

Social and cultural pressures

In a world where social norms often dictate behavior, saying "no" can be perceived as rude or disrespectful. Many cultures and societies teach individuals that agreeing to requests is the expected response. This expectation pressures individuals to comply, even when it violates their personal boundaries or priorities.

For example, in many social settings, saying "yes" is equated with being cooperative and gracious, while saying "no" can be seen as confrontational or selfish. This pervasive belief poses significant challenges for those trying to establish and maintain their own boundaries.

Why Saying No is Saying Yes to More

Increased Focus

Saying no is a powerful tool that greatly increases focus. It simplifies the process of prioritization, making it easier to identify and devote time to high-impact activities. With fewer tasks competing for attention, it's easier to figure out which tasks best align with long-term goals.

This clarity allows individuals to allocate more resources to essential activities rather than diluting their efforts on multiple fronts. Entrepreneurs, busy professionals, and students can all benefit from this form of prioritization to ensure they are working on what really matters.

When commitments are reduced, the risk of feeling overwhelmed is greatly reduced. Over-commitment often leads to stress and burnout, which reduces overall productivity and satisfaction. Individuals can create space in their schedules by saying no to non-essential tasks.

This space helps maintain mental health and stable energy levels, providing a strong foundation for sustained productivity. Simplifying one's schedule by selectively saying no acts as a preventative measure against accumulating stressors and distractions.

Your Action Plan for Saying NO

Clarify your priorities

Understanding what is truly important to you begins with a deep dive into your core values. These principles shape your actions, your decisions, and ultimately, your life. Your core values can range from family and health to professional achievement and personal growth.

Identifying these values requires introspection and honesty about what makes you feel fulfilled and satisfied. Take time to reflect on your past experiences and note the moments that made you happiest or proudest. Patterns in these reflections can reveal your true values.

Set clear, achievable goals

Setting clear, achievable goals that align with your values is the next critical step. These goals serve as milestones that guide you toward living in alignment with your core beliefs and aspirations.

Begin by translating your values into specific, measurable goals. For example, if one of your values is continuous learning, you might set a goal to read a certain number of books each month or enroll in a course that will enhance your skills.

Achievable goals provide a roadmap that directs your efforts and keeps you motivated. It's important to make sure these goals are realistic and achievable within a set time frame. Setting SMART (Specific, Measurable, Achievable, Relevant, Time-bound) goals helps to break down larger ambitions into manageable tasks. This method reduces overwhelm and keeps you focused on steady progress, not just the end result.

Regularly reviewing and adjusting your goals keeps them relevant and in line with your evolving values. Life changes, and so do your priorities and circumstances. By regularly reviewing your goals, you can make the necessary adjustments to ensure that you're always working toward what's most meaningful and important to you at any given time.

Evaluate the ask

Evaluating the alignment and impact of requests is critical to maintaining focus on your goals. The first step in this process is to determine if the opportunity aligns with your established goals. Consider whether the request supports the goals you have clearly defined for yourself.

For example, if one of your primary goals is to improve customer satisfaction within your organization, a request that involves working on a new marketing campaign may be a good fit. On the other hand, if the request deviates from those goals, it's important to recognize that accepting it could lead you astray.

Once you've examined how closely the opportunity fits with your existing goals, it's beneficial to consider how it fits into your broader vision. This includes not only looking at the immediate benefits, but also understanding the long-term implications. Consider past experiences where accepting misaligned opportunities resulted in wasted time or resources. Aligning with your goals will ensure that every decision moves you in the desired direction, ultimately leading to greater productivity and success.

Practice saying no

Practicing saying no in different scenarios can greatly increase your comfort and confidence. Start by identifying situations where you often find it difficult to say no to requests.

For example, if you frequently agree to take on additional responsibilities at work despite your already busy schedule, try rehearsing specific phrases that clearly communicate your inability to do so. Practicing these responses out loud or role-playing them with a friend can help you get used to using them naturally when the need arises.

Another effective strategy is to practice saying no in front of a mirror. This allows you to observe your body language and facial expressions and make sure they match your words.

Practice different scenarios, such as declining a social invitation or turning down a volunteer opportunity. Over time, this rehearsal will make you more comfortable and help you say no with confidence and without hesitation.

Adjust your approach

Adjusting your approach based on what works best in different contexts is essential to mastering the art of saying no. Not every situation requires the same response, so it's important to be flexible and adjust your strategy accordingly.

For example, saying no to a request from a close friend may require a different approach than saying no to a request from a manager at work.

Experiment with different techniques and see how they affect the outcome. Being more direct and concise works well in professional settings, while offering a brief explanation is more appropriate in personal situations. The key is to strike a balance between assertiveness and empathy, ensuring that your rejections are clear yet considerate.

In some cases, delaying tactics can be effective. If you're unsure about a request or need time to consider its implications, don't hesitate to ask for some time to think about it.

Phrases such as "Let me check my schedule and get back to you" or "I'll have to think about it and let you know" can provide the breathing room you need to make a thoughtful decision. This approach not only buys you time, but also shows respect for the other person's request.

Build confidence with practice

Start small by saying no to smaller requests to build your confidence. By starting with less significant requests, you can practice saying no without feeling overwhelmed. For example, the next time a colleague asks you to attend another long meeting that you know is not critical to your role, politely decline. By starting small, you won't feel as much pressure or fear backlash, making it easier to gain confidence over time.

Consider saying no to mundane interruptions. If a coworker asks you for a favor that will take more time than you're willing to give at the moment, tell them that you can't help now, but maybe later. This helps to gently but firmly reinforce your boundaries and contributes to a growing comfort level with the practice of saying no. Consistent small refusals make the act of saying no less daunting.

Once you are comfortable with small refusals, gradually move on to more significant requests. This step-by-step approach ensures that you are not suddenly thrust into situations where you have to say no to larger requests before you feel ready. With consistent practice, you will become more adept at knowing when to say no and how to say it with confidence.

Use Templates or Phrases

Use pre-written templates or phrases for common rejection scenarios. Having a set of responses can take the anxiety out of saying no on the fly. For example, you can use templates such as "Thanks for thinking of me, but I can't commit right now" or "I appreciate the opportunity, but I need to prioritize my current projects.

These templates serve as mental bookmarks, allowing you to quickly and effectively communicate your inability to take on an additional task. Over time, you can tweak these phrases based on past experiences to better suit different contexts and people. Ready-made phrases help streamline your declinations, making them less stressful and more consistent.

Incorporating these templates into your daily vocabulary can also significantly reduce decision fatigue. When you're not constantly coming up with new ways to say no, you free up energy for more important tasks. This simplification increases your productivity by keeping your cognitive load low.

Recognize that saying no is a form of self-care and an essential part of setting boundaries. Understanding the importance of personal boundaries can change your perspective on saying no. When you say no, you are protecting your time, energy, and mental well-being, all of which are critical to staying focused and productive.

Self-care isn't just about pampering yourself; it's fundamentally about making choices that benefit your overall well-being. Saying no to unnecessary commitments prevents burnout and preserves your enthusiasm for the work that really matters to you. It's an affirmation of your value and a recognition that you have limited resources to expend.

By framing saying no as a self-care practice, you align it with positive connotations rather than viewing it as a negative action. You foster a healthier attitude toward setting boundaries, which makes it easier to implement in various aspects of your life. This shift in perspective is essential to maintaining long-term habits.

Use these strategies consistently to form a habit. Habits are formed through repeated actions, and saying no is no different. Consistency is the key to making saying no part of your routine. The more you practice, the more natural it becomes, reducing hesitation and discomfort.

Make it a point to reflect on each experience of saying no. Consider what worked well and what didn't. Did you feel confident? Was the other person understanding? Reflecting on these outcomes allows you to adjust and refine your approach, tailoring it to what feels most comfortable and effective for you.

Over time, your ability to say no will improve and become a seamless part of your interactions. Consistent practice not only builds your skill, but also reinforces your priorities and strengthens your boundaries. As with any skill, persistence and patience are essential.

Consistent use of this framework helps build confidence and the habit of saying no, which leads to better focus and reduced SOS.

Ultimately, the ability to say no is a powerful tool for maintaining focus and avoiding distractions. Embrace this skill as a way to live more intentionally and ensure that every decision you make supports your journey toward achieving your most important goals.

Conclusion: Empowering Your SOS *Freedom Journey*

In "Do the Hard Things First: Defeat Shiny Object Syndrome," we've addressed the pervasive problem of constant distraction and its detrimental effect on our productivity and personal satisfaction.

This book has provided a comprehensive framework for understanding and overcoming Shiny Object Syndrome (SOS), equipping you with practical strategies and tools to regain your focus and achieve your goals.

Now, you have the confidence, knowledge and framework for taking total charge of your life, your business, and your future.

Now, you can create the lifestyle you want instead of sinking in an environment of chaos and uncertainty.

Here is a brief overview of what we have covered in *Do the Hard Things First: Defeat Shiny Object Syndrome—*

Summary of Key Concepts in this book:

1. **Understanding Shiny Object Syndrome (SOS)**

- Introduction and impact of SOS

- Why we focus on shiny new objects

2. **The Role of Dopamine and Social Conditioning**

- Dopamine's role in distraction

- Social conditioning and its influence

3. Scoring and Recognizing SOS

- The 50-point SOS assessment

4. Mindset Traps and Overcoming Them

- Identify common mindset traps (Sunk Cost Fallacy, FOMO, FOBO, Multitasking)
- Strategies for overcoming each trap

5. Prioritizing techniques and improving focus

- Time Blocking
- Implementing the POWER Framework

6. Creating a Focused Work Environment

- Creating a distraction-free environment
- Cultivating a Deep Work Mindset

7. Decision-Making Tools

- Using Decision Trees
- The power of saying no

8. Maintaining Motivation and Ending Procrastination

- Techniques for Staying Motivated
- Strategies for Ending Procrastination

9. Overcoming Multitasking and Removing Temptations

- The myths of multitasking

With this framework, you are now an unstoppable beast. But you need to continue practicing the method so that you stay on track. When you find yourself reaching for those shiny things that threaten to pull you into the land of chaos, you have this training to lean into. Remember what you have learned here, and you'll be fine.

Final Message

Your journey to overcoming Shiny Object Syndrome isn't just about eliminating distractions; it's about fostering a mindset that prioritizes meaningful work and personal fulfillment. Consistently applying the strategies discussed in this book will help you build resilience to distractions and stay committed to your long-term goals.

Remember, the power to control your focus and achieve your highest potential lies within you. Stay disciplined, apply the tools and techniques you've learned, and continually reflect on your progress.

Your journey to a more productive, purposeful, and fulfilling life begins now. Take control, stay focused, and let your true potential shine.

Until then, stay true to who you want to become...focus in on your one thing and stay resilient until you get it done.

Your destiny is in your own hands.

It always has been.

You've got this.

Scott Allan

www.scottallanbooks.com

"If there are nine rabbits on the ground, if you want to catch one, just focus on one."

– Jack Ma

The **Do the Hard Things First**
Series Titles

DO THE HARD THINGS FIRST

Now available for direct purchase at
ScottAllanBooks.com

About Scott Allan

Scott Allan is an international bestselling author of 35+ books published in 16 languages in the area of personal growth and self-development. He is the author of **Fail Big, Undefeated,** and **Do the Hard Things First**.

As a former corporate business trainer in Japan, and **Transformational Mindset Strategist**, Scott has invested over 10,000 hours of research and instructional coaching into the areas of self-mastery and leadership training.

With an unrelenting passion for teaching, building critical life skills, and inspiring people around the world to take charge of their lives, Scott Allan is committed to a path of **constant and never-ending self-improvement**.

Many of the success strategies and self-empowerment material that is reinventing lives around the world evolves from Scott Allan's 20 years of practice and teaching critical skills to corporate executives, individuals, and business owners.

You can connect with Scott at:

hello@scottallan.me

https://scottallanbooks.com/

Scott Allan

Master Your Life One Book at a Time.

<u>Subscribe</u> to the weekly newsletter for updates on future book releases from Scott Allan.

DO THE HARD THINGS FIRST

BY SCOTT ALLAN

Printed in Great Britain
by Amazon

47364259R00108